To: Adam
1-15-12

Adam, you have to remember that God is always there for you and with you. In times of glory & during trials & tribulations. Our trials are tasting of God's and he uses to build and a time with him. our relationship with that God so loved you that he gave is only begotten Son. I love you!
Mom

There's no such thing as a "self-made" man. We are all created by God and the sooner we get in touch with the creators plan the better are time here on earth will be.

love
Glenn

MAX OUT

BY
BEN CRAWSHAW &
DALE CRAWSHAW

"Train yourself to be godly."
1 Timothy 4:7

We want to Thank:

Our super artists and graphic artists:
Tim Williams
Kim Waggoner
Faith Ridley
Stephen Parris
Georgia Design & Graphics, Inc.

Our insightful editing team:
Penny Harman
Gloria Spencer
Suzi Coleman
Natalie Crawshaw
Karly Harman
David Mason
T.J. Stewart
Emily Thompson
Anne White
Whitney Williams

Our gifted senior editor, Rachel Crawshaw

Copyright© 2000 Ben and Dale Crawshaw.

All scripture quotations, unless otherwise indicated, are taken from the HOLY BIBLE, NEW INTERNATIONAL VERSION. NIV. Copyright 1973, 1978, 1984 by International Bible Society. Used by permission of Zondervan Publishing House. All rights reserved.

Scripture taken from The Amplified® New Testament, Copyright© The Lockman Foundation 1954, 1958, 1987 Used by permission. (www.Lockman.org)

ISBN 1-928554-02-4

DEDICATION

I was tired. I'd knocked on about 3,000 doors in a three-year period, sharing Christ with whomever would listen. Most people weren't interested.

Then I met Justin who was visiting Miami on spring break. Instead of slamming the door in my face, he hesitated a second, then smiled and invited me in. I could tell by his searching questions that he was hungry for answers and truth he could live by.

The next few days we spent every possible moment together--hours of questions, hours of searching God's Word for answers. Finally all of his doubts were satisfied. He invited Jesus Christ into his life.

I wish I'd had something to place in his hands that would have helped him pursue the radical Christianity his heart cried out for.

I don't know where you are, Justin, but I dedicate this book to you.

(Dale, Ben's dad, uses the above font throughout the book.)

I was tired, too, but not because I'd knocked on 3,000 doors to share Christ. I had spent the first eighteen years of my life desperately trying to please others and had done a pretty good job. But while the people around me seemed happy, I was miserable, hurt, and confused. I had been raised in a great Christian home and a great church, but somewhere along the line missed the joy of an active, growing relationship with the Lord. It was only when I reached ultimate exhaustion that I said, "Lord, I quit fighting. Take my life and make it what you want." The Lord began a change in me that continues today.

As I began learning the principles that Dad and I talk about in this book, I wondered, *Why didn't I get these in my early teens? Were people trying to tell me? Was I too rebellious to listen?* I'm glad I'm learning these things now, but it is with passion that I say I wish I'd learned them much earlier.

It doesn't matter how young or old you are. It doesn't matter what you've been through. If you are ready to say, "Lord, take my life and make it what you want," I dedicate this book to you.

(Ben uses the above font throughout the book.)

DON'T

...GO ANY FARTHER: READ THIS FIRST!

COACH'S INSTRUCTIONS

Listen up. What we're about to tell you is important. We have a few things in this book we want you to pay special attention to.

One of the writers of this book is Ben Crawshaw (he's the Generation-X, edgy, wild and crazy son). Whenever Ben talks, you will see this and the font will look like this.

The other writer is Dale Crawshaw (he's the middle-aged, sometimes corny, but also wild and crazy, dad). Whenever Dale talks you will see this, and the font will look like this. In parts of the book, they have dialog.

When Dale & Ben share biblical principles together, the font will look like this. Got it? Good!

Next: REPETITIONS-

All you exercise people know that when you have certain muscles you want to develop, you target that area by doing repetitions (called "reps" in body-building language). We have reps inserted throughout the book. They are verses you can write down and learn in order to build your faith muscles. The only absolute truth in this world is the Bible, so flood your mind with its words.

Next: DAILY MAXIMS-

At the end of each chapter, we have affirmations of truth that you can say out loud. Write them down and put them in a place where you will see them daily. Like a pep talk the coach gives before a game, these are positive truths to replace the negative attitudes you've been carrying around.

Finally, for an INTENSE WORKOUT-

try the Study Sheets at the back of the book. They are filled with a variety of exercises that will conform you to the image of Christ. He's our model.

Do you think you can handle it?

We know you can! Pray that the Lord will teach you, through this book, what He wants you to learn.

NOW, GO FOR IT!

TABLE OF CONTENTS

CHAPTER ONE 1
   Maximum Grace

CHAPTER TWO 11
   Maximum Desire

CHAPTER THREE 33
   Maximum Faith

CHAPTER FOUR 55
   Maximum Knowledge

CHAPTER FIVE 75
   Maximum Conditioning

CHAPTER SIX 99
   Maximum Perseverance

CHAPTER SEVEN 121
   Maximum Leadership

CHAPTER ONE

Maximum Grace

I used to be a Craig wanna-be, but one day that abruptly changed. Craig was three years older than I was and very popular in high school. He was a three-sport star athlete and also good enough at fishing to be a professional guide. At that time, being friends with Craig was my goal in life.

A lot of Saturdays, I was up at daybreak. Craig and I would fish all morning in the back country near the Mangrove Islands in the Florida Bay. After a swim to cool off, we'd zip through Whale Harbor Channel and out to the Gulf Stream to catch the big fish. As soon as we'd dock our boat and take our catch to be iced down, we'd go cast fishing on the flats until after dark.

All that just to be like Craig!

One afternoon I learned what it felt like to be the bait instead of the fisherman. We were a mile offshore in Craig's 16-foot skiff, heading out to sea. That's when I noticed something very scary staring at me.

A hammerhead shark every bit as big as our boat was swimming along right next to us. Hammerheads are so-named because their heads are capable of smashing a boat with one mighty thrust.

At the moment, however, it seemed content to torture us. When we carefully turned our boat, it followed. When we would speed up or slow down, it would do likewise. Its eyes, like all hammerheads, were located on the outer ends of its T-shaped head.

Every time I looked over at the monster from my seat in the boat, one of its huge eyes was eerily staring at me.

Talk about sizing up your lunch! I wondered if it was thinking, *Is this the main course or just dessert?*

We turned a very slow circle back toward shore. The big fellow followed. Whenever I dared to look, it was still staring at me. I felt like death was stalking me, and it was terrifying.

As you can imagine, all this seemed like an eternity. We finally got into shallow water, and the tip of our outboard scraped the muddy bottom. The shark's massive bulk began to scrape bottom as well. It was about to ground itself.

In water only deep enough for us to go a few feet further, the shark finally stopped. It thrashed wildly, turned sideways and readied itself to head back out to deep water. But before it did, it took one last long look at Craig and me, as if to say, "Lunch together some other day, fellas."

My love for fishing took a huge setback that day. For weeks I'd wake up in the middle of the night and look out the window toward the dark ocean. I knew the eye of that gigantic hammerhead shark was watching me. When I'd turn away, I'd feel it glaring at my back.

I wondered over and over, "If I were to die, what would happen to me? Where would I spend eternity?"

Soon after that hammerhead encounter, my high school buddy, Scottie, was killed in a shark attack. Was I supposed to be getting some kind of message from all of this? I was certain I'd never go to the reefs again. But when you are raised on the ocean, it's hard to stay away. After quitting cold turkey for a year, I somehow regained my courage to dive once more.

Not long after I started diving and surfing again, another huge shark invaded my life. It was an aggressive ten-foot bull shark that circled three of us as we were diving on Hens and Chickens Reef (and believe me, we were the chickens!).

We barely made it to our boat before it closed in on us. I'll never forget lying in the bottom of the boat, shaking so hard my legs refused to move me to the driver's seat to take us out of there. We finally got going, but more than ever I was sure death was after me. In the weeks that followed, I saw shark in my mind day and night. Scottie had been killed on the reef just north of the site of my close encounter, and both incidents haunted me.

In my mind, I was no longer the big man on campus, the star athlete, the daredevil who would attempt almost anything. I was a frightened sixteen-year-old with an overwhelming fear of death.

So I was ready to listen when someone shared the good news of Jesus Christ with me a couple of months later. That near-death experience helped me to really listen when I heard, "God so loved the world that He gave His one and only Son, that whoever (and that included me) believes in Him shall not perish but have everlasting life." John 3:16

I was made aware of my own mortality and my need for answers to my questions regarding death and the afterlife. The Bible's answers became personal when I inserted my own name:

> "For it is by grace (undeserved mercy!) you (Dale) have been saved through faith – and this not from yourselves (Dale can't help save Dale, only Jesus Christ can do it), it is a gift from God – not of works, so that no one can boast (brag about being good enough to help God pay for sins.)" Ephesians 2:8-9

I realized for the first time that Jesus Christ is a Savior. I was drowning in sin and guilt, and Christ, through his death on the cross, was reaching a hand out to me. My part was to accept, by faith, the forgiveness He was offering me. He would then put me in His lifeboat and take me all the way to the shore of Heaven. Just like a drowning person is rescued on the basis of need alone (no character references or credit checks ahead of time), God, in His grace, doesn't rescue on merit. His gift of salvation is one I don't earn; I just receive.

> "I write these things to you (Dale) who believe in the name of the Son of God so that you (Dale) may know that you (Dale) have eternal life." 1 John 5:13

I was sixteen years old when someone told me the good news of the Gospel. I trusted Christ as my Savior and was instantly freed from the fear of death that had been plaguing me. I felt so excited and so liberated, I wanted to tell everyone this wonderful news. I said, "God, my life is yours. I want to live every day like Jesus would live it, way beyond my own selfishness and natural impulses, and honor You with everything I say and do." God saved me. I wanted to serve Him. I still do.

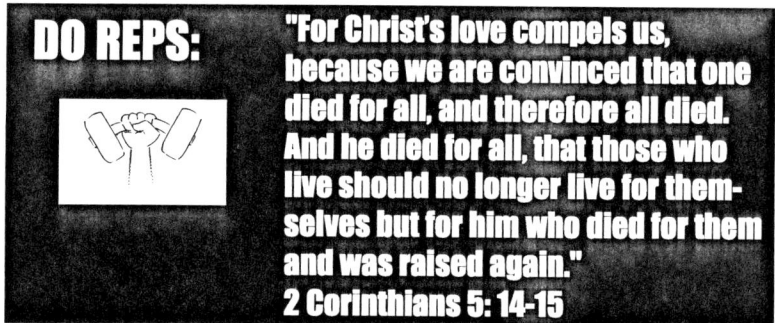

DO REPS: "For Christ's love compels us, because we are convinced that one died for all, and therefore all died. And he died for all, that those who live should no longer live for themselves but for him who died for them and was raised again."
2 Corinthians 5: 14-15

Really

good
won't be
good enough
for you
to earn God's
perfect heaven.

I was in a pretty good mood. I had just pitched a shutout in the last baseball game of my college junior season. I figured that would be great news to Mom and Dad, so I called home that Friday night. But the big news came from them, and it was tragic. One of my high school buddies had just been killed in a car crash.

I was sobered by the report. Corey was dead at nineteen years old.

I'd known him since I was ten. We'd been on the same little league teams. Then, in high school, we'd played varsity basketball and baseball together. The news of his death left me stunned. Somebody I knew so well wasn't supposed to die. Corey and I hadn't been best friends, but I could remember Friday nights when we went to our high school's football games together. Sometimes he and other buddies would spend the night at my house. It was no exaggeration that he was the life of the party and people were drawn to him. Now I was shocked by the news and didn't know how to react.

A couple of weeks later, my high school baseball coach and I began to talk about Corey and how someone so young could die. He said Corey was the third baseball player he had buried in five years of coaching.

It was awful to hear such sad news. It reminded me of the tragic fact that life can end at any time. But even more tragic would be to die and not be sure where you're going.

I'm only twenty-one years old, and several of my friends have already passed away. Some I know were sure of Heaven and some I have doubts about.

If I could go back in time and talk to them before their deaths, I'd be sure to tell them that Jesus died on the cross for them and took their sins away; that if they'd "confess with (their) mouth Jesus is Lord, and believe in (their) heart God raised Him from the dead, (they) would be saved." (Romans 10:9) I would tell them Heaven is wonderful, and salvation is the greatest thing offered in this life.

What if they told me they would just wait until they were older to accept Christ? Later would be too late for them.

People I've failed to share Christ with are big reasons for this book. I don't want to live a sheltered Christian life where I'm ashamed of my faith. No one wants to be around a coward. I want to live my life to its fullest potential, to the MAXIMUM. I hope you want that, too.

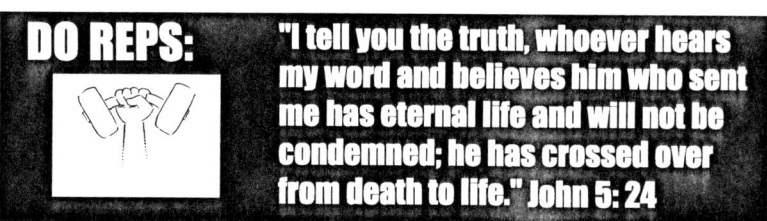

DO REPS: "I tell you the truth, whoever hears my word and believes him who sent me has eternal life and will not be condemned; he has crossed over from death to life." John 5: 24

If you don't know for sure that you would go to Heaven if you died, why not get that settled? Repeat this prayer out loud right where you are: "Dear Lord Jesus...I know that I have sinned...I know sin will keep me out of Your Heaven. But I believe that Christ made the complete payment for my sins when He died on the cross and rose again. I accept You as my personal Savior...This very moment I ask You to forgive me of all my sins—past, present and future...Thank You for loving me."

Do that, my friend, and you are supernaturally born into God's family.

> "Yet to all who received Him, to those who believe in His name, He has given

the right to become children of God..."
John 1:12

All of you who just prayed that prayer, or who have previously done so, please come with us on a journey to a life so awesome you can't even imagine it. We are going to go step by step and learn together how to walk with God.

Eternal life is Maximum Life. It lasts forever. But we don't have to wait until we get to Heaven to start enjoying God's blessings. As we get stronger and learn the principles taught in this book from God's word, we can "take hold of the life that is truly life" (I Timothy 6:17-19).

God's grace is offered freely to all who believe.

It's available to you.

Think of it!

Now you can really live!

DAILY MAXIMS FOR GRACE

- **I am forgiven.** Colossians 1:13-14
- **I am free forever from condemnation.** Romans 8:1
- **I am God's dearly loved child.** John 1:12; Romans 8:14-16; 1 John 3:1-3
- **I am a recipient of God's lavish grace.** Ephesians 1:7-8

CHAPTER TWO

Maximum Desire

It was the biggest wave I had ever ridden.

Two friends and I had gone five miles out in our sturdy twenty-five foot boat to a reef off the Florida Keys. The wind was howling and the seas were rolling. When we saw those monstrous waves, all of us plunged into the water and mounted our surfboards.

My stomach tightened. Reef surfing was dangerous. If you got knocked off your board you'd tumble over sharp coral fingers just a few feet beneath the surface. Besides the pain, blood from the resulting cuts were a dinner bell for sharks that prowled the area. But knowing the dangers only increased the rush.

I caught the wave, and it was huge. Riding the crest, I could see miles of the Key's coastline. Adrenaline flowing, I felt invincible. As a high school student I often felt that way. My whole life was before me, and although I knew there would be pitfalls, I didn't plan on encountering them.

I had recently accepted Christ as my Savior. I wanted to give my life to God for whatever He wanted to do with me. I had been so hungry to hear the good news of the Gospel that I immediately decided to dedicate my life to God.

"That's me," you say. "I want to live out my passion for God. But where do I start?" Start by realizing that if you desire things rather than God, your desire for God will be neutralized.

DO REPS:  "Show me your ways, O Lord, teach me your paths; guide me in your truth and teach me, for you are God my Savior and my hope is in you all day long." Psalm 25:4

"I'm sorry, Junior, but it looks like we're gonna have to move into a house we can afford."

My dad delivered that crushing blow to me one day after school. I knew exactly what that meant. One, we weren't making as much money as before, and two, we'd be living in a smaller house.

I was devastated. As an eighth grader, the last thing I wanted to do was leave the house my dad had built. Nobody in his or her right mind would have wanted to leave that place. It was a huge, two-story house, spread over 4500 square feet with big rooms, a big yard, big everything.

What I loved most was the game room upstairs next to my bedroom. I had just thrown a party there for all my friends, and I was still relishing the compliments I'd received. I felt like the house was my house and nobody else's. The problem with a house that big, and the part I didn't bother to worry about, was how much it cost to maintain. Fact is, funds were dwindling. Just six months before, our family had been living well, paying all the bills, traveling, buying things. We weren't abusing God's blessings, but we were becoming used to having what we needed. Then the problems began.

If you remember the Persian Gulf War, you might recall the havoc it wreaked on the American economy. Gas prices went up, inflation increased and finances became unstable. My dad owned a construction company, and the economy showed no mercy on his business. Nobody was building or buying a house. Nobody! With construction dead so was my dad's company and our income.

I took it as a personal blow to my pride. I was just starting to fit in at school. This would spoil everything. Where was God in all this anyway? I mean, it was His job to take care of us, right? How could He let this happen?

I felt like I was losing a close friend, or even worse, my own precious life. I envisioned those same friends that had come to my party and hung out with me laughing and making fun of me for being poor, branding me a loser.

Despite my selfish attitude, the Lord began to work in me. We moved into a house about half the size of our old one. Then, the next year, when we couldn't afford that, we moved into a double-wide trailer.

So here I was, about to start my sophomore year in high school, and I had just migrated from what I thought to be American success to trailer trash.

Oh, great, I thought, *looking at my new mini-home, This is really gonna impress the girls.*

It was a hard time in my life, but I lived through it. And instead of shaking my faith in God as I expected, the experience actually helped me to discover it. That was the first small step in God beginning to change my desires.

I discovered that girls didn't judge me because of where I lived. I was still Ben. And my friends were gonna be my friends regardless. If they weren't, then they weren't true friends to begin with.

More importantly, I learned I didn't need possessions to be happy. I didn't have to show off in nice clothes or with expensive things. For the first time in my life, I could thank God for the things I had. It made our family grow closer.

I have now grown to love our little trailer, and I'm constantly reminded that what I really need is God—not possessions, not the admiration of every person I see, but God.

What about you? What's your situation? Do you live in a big house or a double-wide? Do you drive a Land Rover or a Datsun? Does it even matter?

According to today's society, the answer is a resounding yes! According to God, absolutely not!

In Luke 12:15 Jesus says, "Watch out! Be on your guard against all kinds of greed: a man's life does not consist in the abundance of his possessions." What you have, whether you're rich or poor, doesn't matter to God.

More money, more clothes, and more friends will not necessarily give you more joy. Let me say it another way: If you look to money, clothes and friends to make you happy, you will be disappointed. The great life God has planned for you doesn't have anything to do with what you own. To Him your life has more meaning than that!

In the Amplified Bible Ephesians 3:20 says:

> "...He is able to carry out His purpose and do super-abundantly, far over and above all that we dare ask or think, <u>infinitely beyond</u> our highest prayers, desires, thoughts, hopes, or dreams."

As a Christian I believed God's grace would one day carry me to Heaven. But my desire to live my life for

God was often overshadowed by my desire to get what I thought I needed to make me happy.

Desire is born from willingness to let God be in charge of our lives. This sounds great in church, but it was a long time before surrender became a part of my vocabulary. I chose willfulness over willingness. God was patient, though. He continued to work through the circumstances in my life, good and bad, to draw me to Himself.

> "...being confident of this, that he who began a good work in you will carry it on to completion until the day of Christ Jesus." Philippians 1:6

In other words, God takes ultimate responsibility for making sure His followers become the people He intends them to be.

NO

My life will not be wasted because living inside me is a God who cannot fail.

BURN THE SHIPS

We now understand that our desire should be focused on what's important to God.

When Julius Caesar sailed over the channel from Gaul and landed in what is now England, he planned for his army to conquer the territory through battle. While his soldiers were on the cliff overlooking the bay in which their ships were anchored, he did an amazing thing. He yelled out, "Burn the ships!"

His men watched in horror as their only link to their homeland went up in flames. When Caesar burned the ships, he eliminated the option of turning back. His men could not get home unless they fought and won. There could be no retreat. Caesar's army became victorious.

We have a much greater cause: to be faithful in what God has called us to do. Realize that fear squelches your desire to please God. Don't cave in.

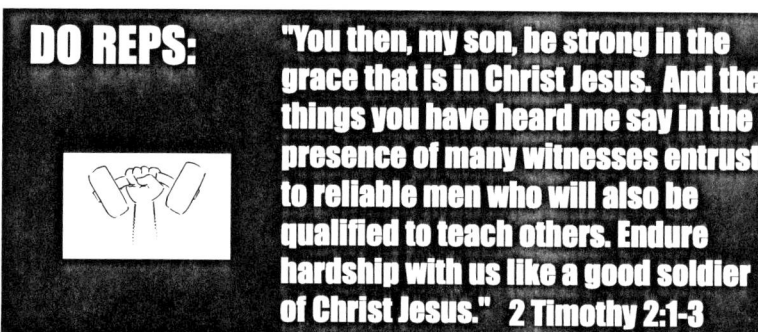

DO REPS: "You then, my son, be strong in the grace that is in Christ Jesus. And the things you have heard me say in the presence of many witnesses entrust to reliable men who will also be qualified to teach others. Endure hardship with us like a good soldier of Christ Jesus." 2 Timothy 2:1-3

When I was sixteen, it seemed like all my ships were burning. During my sophomore year, I'd goofed off and gotten so many low grades that I found myself academically ineligible for sports. That meant my junior year I had to try out for the baseball team with the freshmen.

I made the team, but I felt microscopic. For one thing, my coach's opinion of me was very low. I hung out with a group of guys he wasn't familiar with and obviously I hadn't shown him I was serious about school. The seven seniors on the team thought I was a goof-off and assumed I would bring the level of the team down.

Nevertheless, I was on the team. I was the backup utility infielder and the number six pitcher.

Now, being the number six starter for the Atlanta Braves would be amazing. Even in college the sixth best pitcher gets a lot of opportunities. But in high school, the number six pitcher doesn't even start JV games. I figured my chances of making it to the mound were comical. It was almost hilarious to think how often I wasn't going to pitch.

But something got into my sixteen-year-old head that I still can't explain. I determined to my trembling self that I wasn't going to give in to defeat. I thought I was good enough to play, so I resolved to pitch so well that when I got into a game the coach couldn't put me back on the bench. And I determined something else. I decided to pray for the guys on my team who didn't like me and be nice to them no matter how they treated me.

By the tenth game of the season, I had pitched three games and worked my way into the everyday lineup. Our team ended up going 23-12 and finishing 8th in the state. But you know what? Playing time wasn't nearly as exciting to me as the fact that I had become good friends with the guys who once disliked me.

I'm not saying desire is going to make you immediately successful, but it will help.

First, decide you won't give up. When I determined not to quit, I didn't know what the outcome would be. There was no guarantee that I would succeed in baseball, but the fact that I continued to go out there every day was a victory in itself.

Second, get a goal. The more I determined to prove myself to that baseball team the less I focused on my problems. My goal was to earn their respect on the field. That overrode any of their insults or any of my setbacks. My goal was stronger than my emotions.

Third, pray. Proverbs 16:3: "Commit to the Lord whatever you do, and your plans will succeed." Despite my lack of spirituality, I still believed in prayer and God responded in His grace.

Being a successful Christian is so much more important than being a successful baseball player. How much more should we set aside doubt to strive for godliness. In Philippians 3:10, Paul says, "For my determined purpose is that I may know Him..."

It's an act of the will. And all it takes is a little desire and a lot of calls to the Lord for help.

WAYS TO INCREASE YOUR DESIRE TO PLEASE GOD:

EXPOSE YOURSELF TO THE WORD

When I was in college I took a course in speed-reading. I took it so I could read the whole New Testament every day, which I did for about a year. That might have been a little radical, but I think it gave me the passion for God that I still have today.

Dad, it might have been a little radical, but that's because you're a sixties, radical kind of guy. I, the complacent child of the nineties, haven't read the New Testament in one day, but I have read it and tried to apply it. I understand how important it is.

READ OR LEARN ABOUT PEOPLE OF FAITH

Biographies and stories of how God has used men and women to accomplish His will have always challenged me. In fact, I love stories of anybody who has made a comeback or overcome insurmountable odds. You know I always root for the underdog in sports.

Yes, you do. But when we feel like underdogs, we've got to remember we've got God on our side. God can help us do things we couldn't do in our own strength. Just look at some of the characters in the Bible. We can read about them and see how God moved on their behalf. They were human beings just like we are. I think that's why God told us their stories—so we could see His power displayed in ordinary people. I often think of my grandfather, who served the Lord for fifty years and of you and mom, who are so consistent in the ministry. It makes me want to leave that kind of legacy.

GET AROUND PEOPLE WHO ARE EXCITED ABOUT THE LORD

In sports you try to surround yourself with athletes who are better than you. Why? Because it makes you work harder and pushes you to a higher level. But I didn't do that in my life—I didn't always surround myself with friends who challenged me to be a better person. I was too passive about who I chose for friends (or shall I say, who chose me).

Junior, it says in Proverbs 13:20 that if you walk with the wise, you'll grow wise, but if you hang around fools, you will suffer for it. So make it a goal of yours to hang around wise people who love God and want to honor Him. Resist the people who think that partying is the way to have fun and fill the void in their hearts. That's a dead-end street.

DON'T FOCUS ON YOURSELF

I used to be a mood-swinger. My life was one big emotional roller coaster ride until I changed my outlook. I learned that it isn't always about me. Instead of going someplace new and thinking, *What can these people do for me?*, I now ask myself, *How can I help? Who can I bless or encourage?* I'm still not perfect, but I'm really working on that area of my life.

That's good because selfishness is so—well, you know, selfish. It drains our joy, because thinking of ourselves leaves no room for thoughts of God. It also sets us up for disappointment because no one else is as interested in us as we are. I think we're both doing better in that area of our lives.

DANIEL'S RESOLVE

Daniel was a guy who watched his ships burn. He was born to nobility and should have grown up to help rule his nation. Instead, as a teenager, they took him prisoner of war to the pagan city of

Babylon. Can you imagine being taken from your rich family who may have been killed in front of you and dropped down into a hostile environment where you had no choices at all? Daniel could have said, "Since I can't control my circumstances, I'm powerless to do anything." But that's not what he did. Daniel's desire to please God brought him:

- *Unusual boldness* – *"But Daniel resolved not to defile himself with the royal food and wine..."Daniel 1:8a*

- *Unusual respect* -- *"and he asked the chief official for permission not to defile himself this way. Now God had caused the official to show favor and sympathy to Daniel..." Daniel 1:8b-9*

- *Unusual success* – *"The king talked with them, and he found none equal to Daniel, Hananiah, Mishael and Azariah; so they entered the king's service. In every matter of wisdom and understanding about which the king questioned them, he found them ten times better." Daniel 1: 19-20*

Daniel became famous and powerful. Is that what made him a success? No, his success was in standing by his resolve, living by his convictions, even though his life circumstances were not of his choosing.

Have you resolved to live a godly life? Significance, love and acceptance can only be found in surrender to God. A joyful life depends 99% on God's grace and 1% on your willingness and obedience. But by withholding your 1%, you deprive yourself of real joy. Realize that your desire is strengthened by your resolve.

PEOPLE

can be arrows to point me to God.

Four years ago, I packed my car and left home for my freshman year of college. With as much preliminary advice as I'd received, I thought I was prepared to be the perfect college student. But I wasn't.

I made new friends right away, but I began to look to them for my self-worth and happiness. I started doing things to gain their approval, things I thought I'd never do. It didn't make me happy. Miserable and hurting, I felt deeply angry. Angry that I was doing things I regretted, angry that I wasn't the student I thought I'd be, and angry that my life wasn't perfect.

It hadn't taken me long to dig myself into a hole. I felt trapped by my foolish choices. But I made one wise decision. I resolved to share my situation with someone who cared.

By the time I got home for Christmas break, I'd built up the courage to open up to my friend, Hall. I knew he'd had similar struggles in the past but he was now serving the Lord. I poured out my whole life to him, sparing no detail. He listened, then showed me some steps to get myself straightened out.

It felt good to get that burden off my chest. After that, I shared my situation with a few others, then finally told my parents.

I returned to school for the second semester with a clean slate, but I was afraid. I knew that unless I surrounded myself with some strong people, I'd end up right back in the hole.

The only Christian fellowship I had was Baptist Student Union, which met every Wednesday night. After approaching a fellow after one of the meetings, I told him a little bit about my situation.

He listened impatiently. When I was finished, he prayed a beautiful prayer and left. I felt hung out to dry, and I never heard from him again.

Okay, I thought, *sorry for bothering you!*

I didn't give up though. I thought of another guy I might approach, a junior I had a lot of respect for. After another Wednesday night meeting, I approached him with the same story.

He listened attentively, gave some great words of encouragement, then prayed for me. I think he had good intentions of staying in touch but was just too busy. Again, I never heard from him after that.

I concluded at this point that I wasn't going to find the spiritual friend I needed. I gave up. But God didn't. One night after the same club meeting, a girl walked up to me and introduced herself.

"Hey, I'm Cindy," she said. "I don't really know you, but the first time I saw you, God laid it on my heart to pray for you. Whatever is going on in your life, I just want you to know that anytime you need to talk or pray with someone, I'll be here."

Wow! I thought. *What a statement—especially from a total stranger.*

Looking back now, Cindy seems the obvious answer to my prayers. But I was so stuck on the idea of being mentored by an older male that I missed a godsend. I thought that either she was strange, or she had a weak pick-up line.

A few weeks later, the club had an emotionally intense meeting. Everyone was gathered around the altar, praying silently. To my embarrassment, I began to cry. I was overwhelmed with loneliness and discouragement.

Oh, no. I thought. *I can't believe I'm crying in front of all these people. This is humiliating.* Right then, Cindy came and put her hand on my shoulder.

She didn't say anything, but I knew she was praying for me. After the meeting, for the third time, I opened up and shared my struggles. Boy, did I hear from her again!

We never did anything socially, but every time I saw Cindy, she asked me how I was doing. She left encouraging notes in my mailbox and on my answering machine. She made note-cards with Bible verses on them pertaining to the things I was struggling with. She didn't worry about what people thought; she simply did what the Lord asked her to.

Summer rolled around and Cindy left to work at a camp while I withdrew from that school and headed home. However, God passed the baton from Cindy to a man in my church named Sam Burgess. On top of four kids and a full-time job, Sam found time to meet with me once a week. Cindy had helped me see straight again and get my life in focus. Sam helped me begin to grow.

God often uses people to channel our desires and give us focus in our lives. I feel that if it weren't for the faithfulness of people like Hall, Cindy and Sam, I would not have turned my life around.

I, too, owe everything to a real-life hero, Roy Rohe. It had been six weeks since I'd gone reef diving with a gigantic shark. As I said earlier, the experience left me deeply shaken and searching for answers to the meaning of life.

Roy came to the Florida Keys from Miami to visit one of my buddies. He invited a bunch of us to go with him to hear a college football star speak that night. A couple of my friends and I decided to go.

After the meeting where we heard how the athlete had found Christ, Roy spent four hours listening to all my doubts about Christianity. *How could salvation possibly be a free gift? How could he be so sure we didn't have to earn it by attending church or keeping all kinds of rules?*

I ran out of questions before the Bible ran out of answers, and around sunrise, I asked Jesus Christ to be my personal Savior.

Roy stayed up all night answering my questions because he was committed to sharing the good news of Christ with me. I found out later that I wasn't the only one Roy had made that kind of sacrifice for. Since he had found the Lord a couple of years earlier, he had determined that everyone who crossed his path would understand the plan of salvation. Money, sleep, and inconvenience were no object.

Roy didn't desert me, either. He checked on me regularly to make sure I was reading the Bible and had found other Christians to help me. He did whatever it took to spur my growth.

The Apostle Paul had that kind of dedication. He said:
> "Though I preach the gospel, I have nothing to glory about. I am compelled to preach. And woe is me if I don't! If I do it willingly, I have a reward, but if against my will, I am still accountable for it."
> 1 Corinthians 9:16-17

Roy's obedience brought me to Christ. Knowing Christ gave me a purpose for living. Having a purpose in life fueled my desire to help others. What about you? Are you anyone's hero? Are you making any sacrifices in order to come alongside of someone who's searching or struggling? Are you surrounding yourself with people who desire to obey God?

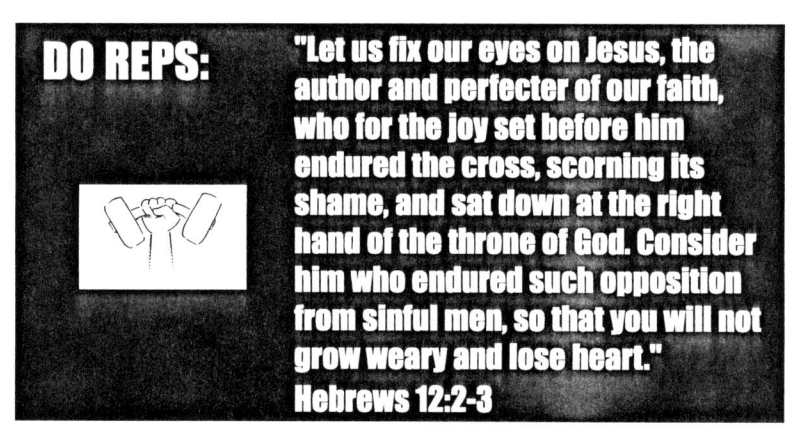

> **DO REPS:** "Let us fix our eyes on Jesus, the author and perfecter of our faith, who for the joy set before him endured the cross, scorning its shame, and sat down at the right hand of the throne of God. Consider him who endured such opposition from sinful men, so that you will not grow weary and lose heart."
> **Hebrews 12:2-3**

We've told our stories of how we came to the point of desiring God's will in our lives. For one of us it came immediately after salvation; for the other it was a long road. We both had people who were passionate for God to help us along the way.

Having a desire to please God will happen only when we understand that He alone can fill the void in our souls. He alone can give us what we really need.

No possession, no popularity, no position can do that. Resolving to be God's man or God's woman wherever we are will give us a desire that will translate into victory day after day.

Desire like that can revolutionize your life.

Determine to live for God.

Be strong and courageous.

Keep your eye on the goal.

Don't quit.

DAILY MAXIMS FOR DESIRE

- **I belong to God.** 1 Corinthians 6:19,20
- **I am fearfully and wonderfully made.** Psalm 139:12-14
- **I have been blessed with every spiritual blessing.** Ephesians 1:3
- **I yield my entire being to the King of kings.** Revelations 1:8; 5:12,13

MAXIMUM DESIRE
MAXIMUM GRACE

CHAPTER THREE

Maximum Faith

DER KOENIG ATHLETEN

The Olympic decathlon is the most demanding athletic test of individual ability. It requires an athlete to compete in ten events. He must sprint one hundred meters, long-jump, heave a sixteen-pound shot, high-jump, race four hundred meters, leap one hundred and ten meters of high hurdles, sling the discus, pole vault, throw the javelin, and finish by running fifteen hundred meters— nearly a mile. The sequence is arranged specifically to prevent him from using the same skill twice in succession. Merely enduring this routine leaves the athlete twelve to fifteen pounds lighter through dehydration.

To win, he must earn top marks under a complicated, seventy-eight page scoring system based on how his performance compares with the latest standard for each event.

The greatest professional baseball, football, basketball or hockey player would be hard-pressed to match a decathlon athlete in stamina or strength. "It would wear out most other athletic stars just to watch a decathlon," claims Dan Ferris, Amateur Athletic Union Secretary Emeritus. That's why in Germany decathlon champions are known as Konig der Athleten—king of athletes.

In 1964, William Toomey, a middle school English teacher from Santa Barbara, California, vowed to win the decathlon in the Mexico City Olympics, four years away. Toomey trained relentlessly in spite of mononucleosis, hepatitis, calcium deposits in his heel, a wrenched back, torn hamstring muscles, a gash in his right calf that required thirty-five stitches, and surgery to remove bone fragments from his right knee.

When he reached Mexico City, Toomey tore a hip muscle before the decathlon got under way. Rules forbid pain-killing drugs, so between events he held an ice pack on the injured area. But he ran harder, leaped and vaulted higher, and threw farther than any of his opponents to win the gold medal at age twenty-nine, the oldest person ever to do so. In the process, he set an Olympic record for total points.

William Toomey, Koenig der Athleten, had something powerful at his disposal—something that takes average, everyday people and makes them great.

"What is it?" you say. "I've got to have it!"

You already do. It's faith. "Now faith is being sure of what we hope for and certain of what we do not see." Hebrews 11:1

Toomey would not have won the grueling decathlon nor even competed had he not believed he could win. No illness or injury dimmed the vision of a gold medal hanging around his neck. Because he had faith, he was willing to do the hard thing. He was willing to endure the pain to reach his goal.

Can't

is no longer
in my dictionary
because
I serve an awesome
God
Who will never be
defeated.

A SOLIDER'S FAITH

Matthew relates an incident where a Roman soldier, a centurion in charge of 100 men, came to Jesus with a critical request. His personal servant was paralyzed and in great pain. (See Matthew 8:5-13)

"I will come," Jesus said immediately.

"I'm unworthy of your presence," the centurion quickly replied, "If you just say the word it will be enough. I am a man under authority, too. I say to this one, go, he goes, or come and he comes."

Jesus was amazed. "I have not found such great faith in Israel."

What made this man's faith greater than others? He really believed Jesus was God. He didn't just recognize Jesus' ability; he recognized Jesus' authority. That is faith.

To become a stable and content person, believe that God can actually change you, change your life. See with eyes of faith. Someone once said, "You live what you believe. All the rest is just religious talk."

Many people trust Christ as their Savior and have surrendered their lives to God, but they still do not have peace and contentment. Why? Because they are on a religious journey, not a spiritual one. They work hard to "succeed" at being Christians, always doing, but for the wrong reasons. They are concentrating on outward behavior; but there will be no long-lasting changes unless they change their core beliefs. What do you really believe about God and how He feels about you?

Does changing our behavior change our beliefs or do our beliefs generate our behavior? Why do we always work on our behavior and not really work on our beliefs?

We attack our own (and others') behavior. Because we give no thought to core beliefs (which determine how we feel and what we do), we stay weak and powerless, living by our emotions.

BEHAVIOR

CORE OF BELIEFS

BEHAVIOR

When we work on believing the truth about who God is and how He loves us, our behavior will come around as we become strong in grace. Work on believing the truth.

"When you were dead in your sins and in the uncircumcision of your sinful nature, God made you alive with Christ. He forgave us all our sins, having canceled the written code, with its regulations, that was against us and that stood opposed to us; He took it away, nailing it to the cross."
Colossians 2:13-14

Nothing you do can make God love you—not your performance, abilities, or even how faithfully you obey the list (Christian rules you live by). He already loves you for free. That's grace. It's like one constant hug from God. So let out a big sigh of relief, tear up your list and enjoy the hug. When you walk by His Spirit, He will enable you to live His life. When you do something that doesn't honor Christ, don't wallow in shame; remember the hug. Then you will become unafraid to be who He created you to be and do what He asks you to do. You will be free to believe God. That's faith.

Whiners

are
not
winners.

> **DO REPS:** "But grow in the grace and knowledge of our Lord and Savior Jesus Christ. To him be glory both now and forever! 2 Peter 3:18

Let me tell you about my sister, Natalie. When she was in the sixth grade, she was small for her age, timid, and struggled with her schoolwork. To top it off she had been born with a hearing loss, so some of her classmates made fun of her. At home, she would cry about these things.

One day she came home from school and our parents excitedly told her that someone had provided hearing aids for her to wear. The last thing she wanted to do was wear hearing aids to school where she already felt out of place. She says that she sat down that night and made a decision that changed her life. She decided to stop feeling sorry for herself. She began to believe that even though there were a lot of things she could not change, she could still be happy.

When she went to school the next day, the first thing she did was announce to her class that she had gotten hearing aids and anyone who wanted to could try them on. Everyone gathered around her, trying on her hearing aids and laughing at how they made things sound. That was a turning point for her.

When Natalie stopped looking at her losses and started believing she could be joyful anyway, she became happier and began to make friends. Today, she is anything but shy and people are constantly gathered around her. She has a glow about her that is attractive to everyone.

Her circumstances didn't change. Her attitude did. She recognized that her problems didn't determine her identity. Nor do yours. You are God's dearly loved child. He has plans for you to give you a hope and a future.

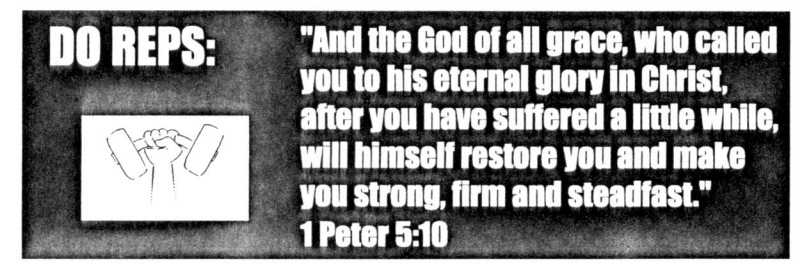

> **DO REPS:** "And the God of all grace, who called you to his eternal glory in Christ, after you have suffered a little while, will himself restore you and make you strong, firm and steadfast."
> 1 Peter 5:10

FLEX THOSE MUSCLES

Like the muscles in our bodies, faith develops through exercise. The person who begins a body building program believes (has faith) for the end result. If you use your faith muscles every day by relying on God for everyday things, you'll find that your confidence in Him consistently increases.

Human reasoning cripples faith. Don't short-change what God can do in your life by self-imposed limitations.

> "Trust in the Lord with all your heart, and lean not on your own understanding; in all your ways acknowledge him, and he will make your paths straight."
> Proverbs 3:5-6

BIG BABY BIBLE LESSON

After my junior year at Lee University, I took a job as a summer intern in Panama City Beach, Florida, for Youth Ministry Resources. This organization put on summer camps for youth groups every week from Monday to Friday. One of my jobs, along with my buddy Aaron, was to lead the high school small group. It was a joke that they called it a small group, because we had over 700 kids in a room with us every day from 11:00 A.M. to 12:00 noon. Over the course of that hour, we played games, Aaron led worship, and I spoke.

One of the messages I gave was titled "Don't Be a Big Baby." Each time I gave the talk, God was showing me the truth about myself. Let me share the main points with you:

The Old Testament outlines the story of the children of Israel, a group chosen by God to be "His people". After many years of slavery under Egyptian rule, the Lord miraculously provided an escape by parting the Red Sea and providing dry land for the people to walk on. As they crossed the Red Sea, they entered the wilderness, where they wandered for forty years. With no food, shelter or medicine, these people were totally dependent on miraculous acts of God to survive. However, despite the Savior's caring hand, these people soon began whining about their lives. As I read their story, I realized that acting like a big baby is warned against in Scripture, and I am a big fat baby myself. Numbers 11:4-6 picks up the story with the children of Israel in the wilderness:

> "The rabble with them began to crave other food, and again the Israelites started wailing and said, 'If only we had meat to eat! We remember the fish we ate in Egypt at no cost—also the cucumbers, melons, leeks, onions and garlic. But now we have lost our appetite; we never see anything but this manna!' "

This manna, or bread, was the food that the Lord provided for these people in the wilderness because they had nothing to eat. It would literally fall from the sky! But the people were getting sick of it, and here's how they responded in verse 10:

> "Moses heard the people of every family wailing, each at the entrance to his tent. The Lord became exceedingly angry, and Moses was troubled."

I want you to picture this: grown men and women outside their tents weeping because of what was for dinner! They didn't care what they looked like to their kids, crying like that. They just wanted meat that they didn't have. **The first sign to know you're a big baby is if you cry when you don't get what you want.**

When I turned sixteen, all I wanted was a new car. But instead I got the four-door family car. This was a tragic event to me, and I became a big baby in a hurry. It hurt relationships around my house for a couple of weeks. I know I cry a lot when I don't get what I want.

It gets worse. Let's look at the next fit they pitched in Numbers 13:31-33;

> "But the men who had gone up with him said, 'We can't attack those people; they are stronger than we are.' And they spread among the Israelites a bad report about the land they had explored. They said, 'The land we explored devours those living in it. All the people we saw there are of great size.'"

Moses, their leader, sent twelve spies to investigate the Promised Land. The reason it's called the "Promised Land" is because the Lord promised the people they could take it. But when the spies brought back a "bad report" about the people in the land, the Israelites quickly forgot His promise along with their dignity.

Here's their response in Chapter 14, verses 1-2:

> "That night all the people of the community raised their voices and wept aloud. All the Israelites grumbled against Moses and Aaron, and the whole assembly said to them, 'If only we had died in Egypt! Or in this desert!'"

The second sign that tells you you're a big baby is if you cry, saying, "Life is too hard." The thing that is amazing about this story is these people were the same people who had seen God part a great body of water right down the middle, just so they could escape across dry land. A cloud led them through the wilderness by day and fire by night! Yet still they doubted God when the spies came back with a bad report.

If you are a Christian, have you seen God do amazing things? I know I've seen God's powerful hand in my own life and in the lives of others. I believe the reason I can still pitch the baseball is because the summer after my freshman year, the Lord healed my shoulder. But today, obstacles appear over the course of my week and I run and hide...something negative happens in the morning and my whole day is ruined! It's just me, crying because life is too hard.

In this last story, the Israelites had just lost a battle, and they came to Moses to ask why. Deuteronomy 1:41-45 tells the story:

> "Then you replied, 'We have sinned against the Lord. We will go up and fight, as the Lord our God commanded us.' So everyone of you put on his weapons, thinking it easy to go up into the hill country. But the Lord said to me, 'Tell them, Do not go up and fight, because I will not be with you. You will be defeated by your enemies.' So I told you, but you would not listen. You rebelled against the Lord's command and in your arrogance you marched up into the hill country. The Amorites who lived in those hills came out against you; they chased you like a swarm of bees and beat you down from Seir all the way to Hormah. You came back and wept before the Lord, but he paid no attention to your weeping and turned a deaf ear to you."

The third sign that tells you you're a big baby is if you cry when you get caught. These people were clearly instructed by God not to go into battle, yet they disobeyed and fought anyway. Then, when they lost, they came crying to Moses, asking him why.

He told them it was their disobedience that had caused the Lord to turn away from them. When you have clear instructions from God, it's hard to find excuses for getting busted. Today, we have the Bible as our instruction manual on what to do and what not to do.

When the choice, "Am I going to cry when I don't get what I want?" comes up, when you feel like life is too hard, or when you're trying to decide whether or not to follow the commands in the Bible and do what's right, read Philippians 4:13, which says, "I can do all things through Christ who gives me strength." This passage is used regularly before sporting events, but I like to use it when I want to be a big baby (which happens a lot), because there is no way for me to fight that without the power of God.

LIVING CONFIDENTLY

Faith is confidence in God, not in circumstances or good feelings. Faith is not a way to get God to do what you want, but it is a willingness to risk everything and trust Him.

Hebrews 3 tells us that the first generation children of Israel never entered the Promised Land because of their unbelief. They couldn't believe God enough to override their emotions.

That's why faith is so important in our Christian lives. It's the hand with which we reach up to grasp things beyond ourselves beyond our knowledge, beyond our capability, beyond our resources, beyond our endurance.

Nearly everything we do in life from expecting our paycheck to turning on a light switch is based on our trust in something or someone. "But," you say, "those are things I have experienced in the past. So I know they'll happen again." True. And God's past performances are all around us as well.

> *"He who did not spare His own Son, but delivered Him up for us all, how will He not also, along with Him, graciously give us all things?" Romans 8:32*

THREE STRIKES AND YOU'RE IN

Now I want to teach you something about faith by giving you a bowling lesson. Yes, bowling. My typical scores are between 170 and 190. Not bad for an old guy! A few months ago my scores dropped into the 150's. Naturally, that made me a very unhappy camper.

I tried a new grip on the ball. I experimented with new approaches and deliveries. Nothing helped. Then one day, I noticed something.

If you've ever bowled, you know there are little arrows on the floor a few feet down the lane. If you stand in the right place and throw your ball over the arrow you've picked, it should go exactly where you want it to go.

I finally figured out that a second before I let go of the ball, I was taking my eye off the arrow and glancing at the pins. Somehow I'd lost confidence in the fact that if I put the ball over the correct arrow, it would hit the pocket in the right place. Since the pins are a lot further away than the arrows, my aim had gone to pot.

So I started talking to myself, "Dale," I said, "you throw the ball over the top of the second arrow or I'm going to beat the snot out of you." I must have gotten my attention because my very next game was over 200! I don't expect that things will always turn out the way I want them to. I may never throw a 300—a perfect game. But that doesn't stop me from trying to beat my high game of 258.

So the bowling lesson for today is: Stay focused.

If that lesson's important in bowling, how much more so in life? Faith means staying focused on God...today. Do what God wants you to do now (watch the arrows). Let God take care of your future (the pins). Have faith for the outcome of your life.

Faith means we do what God tells us to do and we keep doing it...holding on to God and what we know about Him and not reacting emotionally. Don't you know people who are happy one day, trusting God, and then they are down in the dumps the next day? They need faith to anchor their emotions.

How are you doing in the game of life? Afraid of circumstances or people or the future? Stop wimping out. Put your faith to work. Go after the head pin of your fears. Tell that problem that in Jesus' name you refuse to allow it to stick it to you.

Fight! Pick up your sword—God's word. Attempt whatever He asks because you have the name and the blood of Jesus. In the name of the Lord, be bold, for He "gives us the victory through our Lord Jesus Christ."
(1 Corinthians 15:57)

DIALOG

HERE ARE SOME WAYS TO BUILD FAITH:

GET THE MIND OF CHRIST THROUGH SCRIPTURE

Romans 10:17 says, "Faith comes from hearing the message, and the message is heard through the Word of Christ." A dose of Scripture today won't carry me through tomorrow. Each day as I read, meditate on, and apply the Word, it revitalizes me and my disposition. It is an injection of faith and joy. I need it so I won't become a grumpy old man.

You'll never be a grumpy old man. Spaced-out, maybe, but never grumpy! It's true; Scripture can improve a person's outlook. Having a quiet time keeps me from being a jerk sometimes. My accountability partner says he does his devotions because he likes the person he is when he does them a lot better than the person he is when he doesn't do them.

LET THE HOLY SPIRIT TEACH YOU

Look at this Scripture. John 14:16-17 says, "And I will ask the Father, and He will give you another Counselor to be with you forever—the Spirit of truth. The world cannot accept Him, because it neither sees Him nor knows Him. But you know Him, for He lives with you and will be in you." Verse 26B adds, "(He) will teach you all things and remind you of everything I have said to you." Isn't that awesome? We have a source of power and help available to us. It would be foolish for us not to use this help.

I agree. Take a look at that Scripture. The Holy Spirit helps us by teaching us and reminding us of things we need to know at the right time. That's like having a coach talking in your ear, telling you what to do, and then helping you do it. Not to take advantage of that would be really foolish!

REMEMBER PAST BLESSINGS

🧑 You know, Pops, how we go to lunch sometimes and talk about some of my old baseball games when I pitched pretty good? Well, those talks inspire me for the outings I have now. They tell me that I was good in the past and I can be good now.

🧑 Yeah, you know how old guys like me love remembering "the good ol' days!" But on a serious note, God repeatedly told the children of Israel to remember what He had done for them in the past and to remind their children. Remembering God's faithfulness and His power gives us confidence in the face of the present difficulty.

COMMUNICATE WITH GOD

🧑 You know what I've been thinking about? I think it is encouraging to go to church. It gets me going—all the praise music, prayer, encouragement from Scripture. I thought, *Why not try to have a daily worship service in my quiet time?* I play or sing praises to God. It reminds me of who God is and makes me more aware of His presence and power. Then I read Scripture, which gives me truth and a battle plan to defeat the enemy. I close by talking to the Lord and trying to listen to what He wants to tell me. Then it's time to go out and encourage others. Pretty good plan, huh?

🧑 You said it. My day begins something like this: My car has no CD or tape player, and my singing voice does not really sound like someone singing. So, after I read my Bible and get in my car, I imagine Jesus riding with me. Whatever I'm feeling, I talk to Him out loud and I think about how He would answer. *Dale, you know bet-*

ter than that. I'll provide all your needs. Or hitting me on the side of the head (playfully, of course), *Straighten up, buddy. That kind of thinking is the exact opposite of what you said in your sermon Sunday.* Then He'll pat me on the back while I talk, like we're best friends.

YOUR NEW BEST FRIEND

Tell God all that is in your heart as you would talk to a dear friend. You could try making two lists. On the first, write things that you can thank God for—the miraculous and the trivial. On the second, list concerns, hopes and dreams – things you need or situations you should commit to the Lord. Review them each time you pray. Praise and gratitude will overwhelm you. Or why not have a worship service in your room or in your car?

Then spend time in stillness. God may speak to you through Scripture or through thoughts. You may sense a closeness to Him as you allow His presence to seep into your soul.

The eleventh chapter of Hebrews gives a role call of Bible men and women who used maximum faith and received maximum results. Can God say as much of us?

> *"By faith, (your name), refused to live by the world's standards, choosing not to seek pleasure, but rather to persevere, because he/she saw Him who is invisible." Hebrews 11:24-27*

Faith rests in God.

Faith believes God.

Faith doesn't wail when life is too hard.

Faith fixes its eyes on Jesus.

Daily Maxims for Faith

- I am free of anxieties, because I am God's personal concern. 1 Peter 5:7
- I will rejoice and hope in Christ who does all things well. Romans 2:22-23; 5:2, 3, 11
- I have direct access to God through the Spirit. Ephesians 2:18
- I can walk in newness of life! Praise the Lord! Romans 6:6-12 & 17-18

CHAPTER FOUR

Maximum Knowledge

"Carla!"

It was the morning after Roy Rohe had taken me to hear a talk by a Christian athlete in Miami and then stayed up all night answering my questions. Only minutes earlier I had asked Jesus Christ to come into my life. I couldn't wait to tell somebody, so I called Carla, the most popular girl in school and a good friend.

"Do you know it's seven o'clock in the morning on Saturday?" she said.

"I know, Carla, but did you know that if you died you could be sure of going to heaven?!"

"Naturally," she said with a bit of irritation. "I've always known that."

"Well, why didn't you tell me?!" I almost shouted.

She was silent for a moment. "I thought everyone knew that."

At that moment I realized two things: there were people who knew this Good News and they weren't telling; and not knowing what the Bible said had caused me a great deal of anguish.

"Now then, my sons, listen to me; blessed are those who keep my ways. Listen to my instruction and be wise; do not ignore it. Blessed is the man who listens to me, watching daily at my doors, waiting at my doorway. For whoever finds me finds life and receives favor from the Lord. But whoever fails to find me harms himself; all who hate me love death." Proverbs 8:32-36

What you don't know can harm you.

Proverbs 4:7 says, "Wisdom is supreme; therefore get wisdom. Though it cost all you have, get understanding." Through Scripture we come to know the mind of God and to develop Biblical insight. When we see the events of our lives, happy or sad, from God's viewpoint, we can better understand God's purposes. Then if circumstances point us in a direction we wouldn't have chosen, our inner security doesn't crumble. We have faith in God's character and in the truths of His word.

NO SUBSTITUTE FOR COMMUNICATION

When I started college I went through my entire freshman year with a crush on a girl and didn't tell her.

On the last day of school—the last day I would attend college there—I packed my car and made a final turn around the campus.

A strange feeling came over me. *I'm gonna tell her how I feel,* the thought snuck into my brain unexpectedly.

I bet you can't, some other side of my mind taunted.

Don't ever tell me I can't do something. I turned my car around and headed toward her dorm.

Wouldn't you know, she was standing right outside the door?

I parked and casually walked in her direction.

"Hey, Ben."

"Hey!"

"You headin' home?"

"Yep. Just wanted to say bye."

"I'm glad you stopped by. I hope you have a good summer."

"You, too. I—wanted to tell you something." I took

a deep breath. "I've kind of had a crush on you all year. I feel like an idiot telling you this. But you have a lot of qualities that have really impressed me. There may be days you feel like it doesn't matter, but I want you to know people notice."

"Ben, you should have told me earlier."

Yeah right, I thought. *For all I know, I might have told her earlier and had to watch her laugh at me.*

"Yeah, I'm a dork," I said. "Well, guess I'll get going now."

She said goodbye, and I left without risking further damage to my self-esteem.

I was frustrated with myself. I lacked charm and charisma, sure, but that girl didn't have a chance to reject me. She didn't have a clue about my feelings until that day. Would it have made a difference? I'll never know. I had kept my feelings from her.

I had done a pretty good job of keeping things from my parents, too. "What they don't know won't hurt 'em," my friends used to say—referring to parents—when we were planning stuff we shouldn't have been into. Looking back, I realize how wrong they were. I didn't see that I was only cheating myself, and if my parents had known what was going on, they would have tried to help.

Finally, I did decide to tell my parents about the real me. And though I revealed things that I had been hiding for a long time, the healing process began immediately.

True knowledge begins with being honest before God and eventually with others: letting them know who we are, what we need, and how we feel.

The next step is to recognize that the things we've always believed about ourselves, about God, about what it takes to be happy, might not be true. Real truth cannot be found apart from God's Word.

> "We are not meant to remain as children at the mercy of every chance wind of teaching and the jockeying of men who are expert in the crafty presentation of lies. But we are meant to hold firmly to the truth in love, and to grow up in every way into Christ, the head."
> Ephesians 4:14-15 (Phillips)

A lot of people won't go to a gym to work out because they will feel embarrassed. Why? They don't want people to see how much they need to work out. Crazy, huh? I mean, who is a gym for, if not for people who need to get in shape?! If I really mean business about getting fit, I need to face the reality of where I am and learn all I can about how to get where I want to go. I need to humble myself. What I learned about weightlifting is that you need knowledge to get the maximum benefit from the exercises. You need proper technique so you don't injure yourself.

It's the same way with the Christian life. You need God's Word as the basis for what you do and how to go about it. You can't take other people's opinions as the basis for your life. Build your life on the truth of the Bible. Go where you can learn more.

You won't have real joy until your heart is committed to truth. He wants you from the inside out, seeking Him on a daily basis, trusting Him with all aspects of your life.

What freedom there is before God in being honest about how you feel! The truth is He loves you; He understands you; He accepts you unconditionally. It's awesome!

God's

truth produces strength in me.

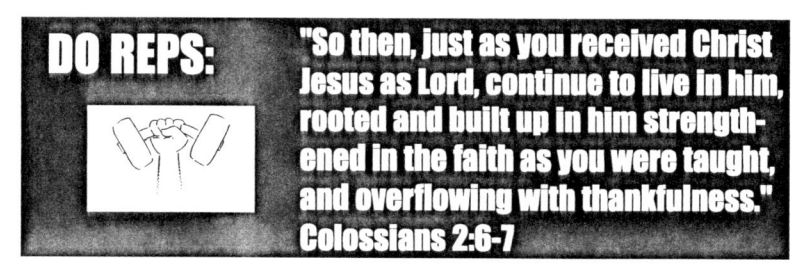

DO REPS: "So then, just as you received Christ Jesus as Lord, continue to live in him, rooted and built up in him strengthened in the faith as you were taught, and overflowing with thankfulness." Colossians 2:6-7

Growing up as a preacher's kid, I quickly learned the ins and outs of Christianity. I knew what a Christian was supposed to do: pray, witness to the unsaved, read the Bible, etc. The only problem for me was I only did them out of guilt.

For instance, if I read my Bible at night, I would usually fall asleep without giving any thought to what I had read.

I more or less slid along on my parent's Christianity until my freshman year in college. I started doing things that my parents, people from my church, and other authority figures in my life didn't know about. I was an eighteen-year-old running from the Lord, and I was already getting tired of my life.

A person can only ignore the Lord for so long. God constantly pursues us until He wins us over or we become so hardened we don't hear Him calling anymore.

When I got tired of fighting, I told the Lord He could have me, the huge mess that I was.

His response? "I'll take you."

With my new-found commitment, I knew my life had to drastically change. So, as soon as I could, I changed colleges, music, dating philosophies (my old one was to pretty much date whoever I was attracted to and actually liked me back), even my hair color. But I soon found that although these things helped me change my lifestyle (all but my hair color), they didn't help me grow as a Christian.

Sure, I grew a little by hearing good messages and having good talks with wise people, but it wasn't the significant growth I wanted.

One day, the summer after my freshman year, Dad came home with a gift for me. A devotional book. *Whoopty-doo!* I thought. But soon I discovered it was not a devotional book, but a spiritual journal that allowed me to keep tabs on the consistency in my devotions.

It was just the thing I needed to get my quiet times on track. The book encouraged everyday Bible reading, prayer, and journaling. I have used the method I learned from that book for two years. The structure of the book keeps me focused during quiet times. (To order journal I have designed, see back of book.)

My sophomore year, I came to realize just how important daily devotions are. I'd transferred to a community college in Florida. I was excited about my developing relationship with the Lord, but that didn't mean everything was perfect.

All the athletes from that school, men and women, lived in the same apartment complex. There weren't many committed Christians and the atmosphere was about as close to Christian as WWF wrestling is to real. Most of the people lived by impulse, not moral code.

I was determined not to make bad choices. However, I had to do it with little encouragement and no one to confide in.

Those were some of the worst times of my life, but some of the best times with the Lord. I'd come to Him barely hanging on. I think He found joy in those times, not because I was struggling, but because I was helpless, which made me dependent on Him.

From those experiences I learned that my relationship with the Lord works like a relationship with anyone else. You have to work at it. You don't have to journal your devotions like I did, and you don't have to wait until your back is against the wall. But you do have to make some sort of daily commitment to spend time with the Lord.

Luke 11:3 says, "Give us each our daily bread." The key word is *daily*. Some days we'll feel like it; some days we won't. There have been times I have used my busy schedule as an excuse for missing my time with the Lord. Then the next day I come into my quiet time and think, *This is so encouraging! Why didn't I find time to do this yesterday?*

The more I learn about God's Word, the more I understand His love and grace, and the easier it is for me to do the things I know are right.

KNOW THE BOOK

Wisdom to make right choices begins with the Word of God. We live in a world that no longer believes in absolutes. As Christians it is comforting to know that we have absolute truth—God's Word. By understanding Scriptures in their context, we begin to understand the mind and heart of God.

Imagine being able to get up every morning, turn on the radio and tune in to a "Live from God" broadcast. Think of all the practical advice, encouragement, and strength you would receive from Heaven.

Actually, we have that opportunity! Everyday we can turn the pages of the Bible and listen to God speak. His wisdom and encouragement is as fresh and relevant as if we were receiving them live from

Heaven.

God's Word is the vehicle through which we learn God's thoughts, feelings and plans so that all of our words, actions, attitudes and motives can line up with His.

Knowing what God's Word says initiates a whole new life in us. It redirects our desires from self-absorbed activity toward eternally lasting endeavors.

REAL RICHES

"The fear of the Lord is the beginning of knowledge..." Proverbs 1:7a *When we get to a point where we respect God and realize just how much we need Him minute by minute, then we have the right frame of mind to acquire wisdom and understanding.*

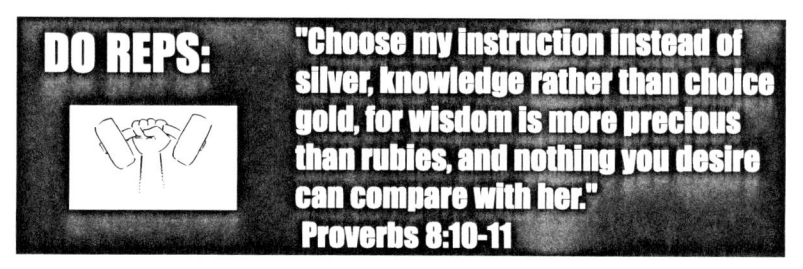

> **DO REPS:** "Choose my instruction instead of silver, knowledge rather than choice gold, for wisdom is more precious than rubies, and nothing you desire can compare with her."
> **Proverbs 8:10-11**

The following list reveals the benefits of getting wisdom and understanding.

Wisdom is:

- *Applying the truth of God's Word. Proverbs 2:6*
- *Knowing Biblical principles for life situations. Psalms 119:11*
- *Becoming honest with God, others and ourselves. Psalms 119:9*
- *Applying our hearts to understanding. Proverbs 2:2,11*

- *Pleasing the Lord with our words and actions. Psalms 111:10*
- *Growing and seeking guidance. Proverbs 1:5*
- *Fearing God. Job 28:12-28*
- *Speaking words of encouragement. Proverbs 16:23-24*

We get wisdom and understanding by:

- *Studying God's Word. 2 Timothy 2:15*
- *Asking God for it. James 1:5*
- *Making them priorities. Proverbs 4:6*
- *Disciplining our minds to study and remember what we learn. Proverbs 4:4-5*

The result of wisdom and understanding is:

- *A blessed life. Psalm 128*
- *Faithful obedience to God without fear. Joshua 1:8-9*
- *A peaceful and joyful life. James 3:13-18*

Accept

a responsibility you're afraid of and say "I can do all things through Christ who strengthens me."

BATTLE GEAR

Ephesians 6:13-18 gives a list of our battle gear:

"Therefore put on the full armor of God, so that when the day of evil comes, you may be able to stand your ground, and after you have done everything, to stand. Stand firm then, with the belt of truth buckled around your waist, with the breastplate of righteousness in place, and with your feet fitted with the readiness that comes from the gospel of peace. In addition to all this, take up the shield of faith, with which you can extinguish all the flaming arrows of the evil one. Take the helmet of salvation and the sword of the Spirit, which is the word of God. And pray in the Spirit on all occasions with all kinds of prayers and requests. With this in mind, be alert and always keep on praying for all the saints."

Are you ready to fight?

DIALOG

PUT ON THE ARMOR

God is all-powerful and all-knowing. Satan, on the other hand, is a defeated foe, but he doesn't want me to know that. His efforts to get me to believe lies are relentless. The only way to resist him is to put on the full armor of God:

THE BELT OF TRUTH—God's Word is true. If it's not according to the Word, it's not true.

BREASTPLATE OF RIGHTEOUSNESS—I choose to honor and glorify God.

SANDALS OF PEACE—I will remind the accuser that

because of Christ, I have peace with God.
SHIELD OF FAITH—I will not be enslaved to anything because I know who I am in Christ. I am not a helpless victim; my situation is not hopeless; God is in control.
HELMET OF SALVATION—My mind is protected by the Holy Spirit as I guard and renew it.
SWORD OF THE SPIRIT—The spoken Word of God pierces the devil's lies.

That's a lot to remember. But since it is the only way to resist the enemy, it is important. I have found that some of this, however, will gradually sink in as you grow in your relationship with the Lord. I didn't understand the entire armor of God at one time. But the Lord showed me, bit by bit, how each one was important to me and the way I live my life.

UNDERSTAND THE ENEMY

Like I said before, Satan is a liar. In fact, he is the father of lies. When negative thoughts come to my mind, I can take them captive by determining whether or not they are true. Earlier in my life, I didn't examine my thoughts. I would entertain them, then feed them by running them over and over until they became arguments. Soon I would believe they were true. Living my life according to those arguments created strongholds. When my mind was full of strongholds—worry, fear, and guilt—it left no room for truth.

I'm a stronghold builder myself. But it says in 2 Corinthians 10:5 we are to "take captive every thought to make it obedient to Christ." That means replacing those condemning thoughts with the truth. I refute out loud, "That is a lie. It is not a truth from the Bible." Then I ask the Holy Spirit to bring a Scripture to my mind, replacing the lie with truth. That's why I'm such a strong believer in Scripture memorization. It is the truth, and our minds are renewed and set free by the truth.

STAND FIRM

I'll tell you one thing I don't want to be: a whining, depressed, self-pitying, stressed-out Christian. God's power is bigger than that! The devil was defeated when Christ died and rose again. I want to "be strong in the Lord." 1 Peter 5:12 tells me to "stand fast" in God's grace. I try to do that every day—picture myself standing in grace—like being in a pool of water with grace up to my neck.

I'll tell you what I don't want to be: a spiritual wuss. I don't want to be a sissy Christian with no backbone. 1 Corinthians 16:13 says, "Be on your guard; stand firm in the faith; be men of courage; be strong." The next five verses talk about laboring with others and being refreshed by them. I have found that one of the best ways to be strong and on guard is by meeting with people who encourage me and tell me the truth. I love it!

PLAN OF ATTACK

My junior year, Aaron introduced me to something that has helped me stand firm in faith—Scripture memorization. If you're yelling, "Scripture memorization?! I do enough memorizing at school!," don't shut me off yet. This is not memorization in order to quote the whole Bible and impress your friends. This is a plan of attack against the things that cause you to struggle.

Aaron knows the things I struggle with, since he is my accountability partner. I'm tempted by something that is common to men—lust. If this freaks you out, it makes me wonder if you live in the same culture I do. Sex and flesh are everywhere. I have three sisters, and I know when I see guys checking them out up and down, left and right, it makes me furious. I told Aaron I didn't want to be that kind of person. So he brought me a list of eleven Scripture verses pertaining to that subject and encouraged me to memorize them. Well, it seemed like it took forever and ever, but I finally learned them. Why is it so important?

It is one thing to have a devotional time, reading Scripture and praying, but taking the words of God into your day is another. I've worked for several summers in Panama City Beach, Florida. I have several jobs that require me to be outside, such as refereeing the basketball tournament. Working outside creates situations that are tempting, but by knowing specific verses on lust, I have artillery to fight the attacks of temptation as they come. For instance, if a girl walks by, I remind myself of the first two verses in the list of eleven:

- "Let your eyes look straight ahead, fix your gaze directly before you." Proverbs 4:25
- "I made a covenant with my eyes not to look lustfully at a girl." Job 31:1

There it is, my weapon—the Sword of the Spirit. Now I don't always win the battles, but with these verses, along with others, it sure has helped.

After I had memorized these verses, I decided to take this concept into other areas of my life. I tend to be a fearful person, so I made a list of ten verses on fear and memorized them. Verses like:

- "Fear of man will prove to be a snare, but whoever trusts in the Lord is kept safe." Proverbs 29:25

🏋 "So do not fear, for I am with you. Do not be dismayed, for I am your God. I will strengthen you and help you. I will uphold you with my righteous right hand." Isaiah 41:10

I figure I'll start now, memorizing Scripture for all the things I will struggle with my entire life. I can do this until I die! Whether that's a long time or not, I know these verses are gonna be a huge help. Why don't you try it? What are your weaknesses? There are Scriptures you can memorize that will help. That's why we have the reps throughout this book. Write them out and start today. You can do it!

God's Word has power. It is living and vibrant. When you begin to see the truth, through the Scriptures, dramatic results are possible. His Word is His love letter to you.

Do you have a passion to know God?

He's pursuing you.

He delights in knowing you.

He's the life you've always longed for.

Daily Maxims
For Knowledge

- **I am alive in Christ.** Ephesians 2:18
- **Knowing God's truth will set me free!** John 8:31, 32
- **I am not shackled by my past.** Colossians 2:13-14
- **I can rest from the burden of trying to manage life on my own.** Hebrews 3: 20, 21

MAXIMUM KNOWLEDGE
MAXIMUM FAITH
MAXIMUM DESIRE
MAXIMUM GRACE

CHAPTER FIVE

Maximum Conditioning

There comes a time when you just have to go to the gym and do it. Sounds easy, right? Not always! Remember when you tried to get in shape? You devised this complicated plan: get off the couch and go run. Why was that so hard? Once you were in shape, getting off the couch was no problem, but the initial action seemed monumental. You didn't have to do it, but you felt a lot better afterwards.

We've talked about grace, desire, faith, and knowledge; now we want to actually work it into our lives—conditioning.

BE ACCOUNTABLE

I'd be a hypocrite if I said I'm an organized guy. If I dared to lie and say I was, my friends would read it, die laughing, and never let me hear the end of it. Fact is, I'm fairly messy, I'm often late, and I tend to do just enough work to get by. Sometimes when I consider the fact that I'm a senior in college, I'm utterly amazed.

But then I force my mind to focus on the positive: First, I am a senior in college. That is a feat in itself. I have a decent GPA, and I'm even considering graduate school. Second, in three years of college baseball, I've only had to run twice for being late.

"Yippee," you say, "You're a real hero. But I've never been late to anything my entire life, and my GPA is closer to 4.0 than yours is to 3.0."

Okay, I'll give you credit. That's pretty impressive. I have friends like you, who are one hundred percent prompt and studious. My parents make me become friends with people like that. I'm probably going to have to marry a girl like that—one who can balance our checkbook and pay our bills in case I forget.

Aaron is that kind of guy. He has a 4.0 GPA and can tell you what he'll be doing at 4:33pm two weeks from now.

I first met Aaron at a summer camp in 1998, but really didn't get to know him until we had a psychology class together my junior year at Lee University. He's one of the nicest guys I know, but he's quite different from me. I learned that one day when our professor gave us our graded tests back. This was a pretty tough test and I noticed Aaron wasn't his usual chipper self. I eased into the conversation to find out why.

"What'd you make there, buddy?"

"An 86."

Good grief, I thought as I looked down at my 64.

"That's a B, Aaron. That's pretty good. Do you usually do better than that or something?"

"That's the worst grade I've made since I've been in college."

I about choked. Here I was, sitting next to a laid-back musician in vintage clothing. The last thing I thought he'd be was a summa cum laude student. He looked more like a hippie. I had figured I'd be helping him with his homework. After that, I realized I'd be needing his help if I was going to get higher than a D in that class.

Over the course of the year, Aaron and I became good friends, and eventually, accountability partners. We began meeting once a week to talk about spiritual matters, a practice we continue today.

One of the things we talk about is time management. I think Aaron has taken it as a personal challenge to get me organized. But he does it for a good reason: it will help my spiritual life.

For instance, if I decide to spend an hour a day of concentrated time with the Lord, that time needs to be set aside. I can't cram my day with activities and no breaks, or I'll never find the time to do it. Also, I can't run so far behind in the things I plan that my hour with the Lord turns into five minutes.

I've made sizable improvements. Each week Aaron and I meet, we ask each other if we've had our quiet times, maintained our bodies with sufficient food and rest, and acted in ways that are pleasing to Christ. The last thing Aaron always asks me is how many hours of study I've put in that week. I'm usually tempted to lie or tell him to leave me alone. But I realize if I want to get organized and accomplish more, an important factor is having someone to hold me to it.

Be accountable. Find a friend to meet with on a regular basis who will question you about schoolwork, devotional time, or anything else you want him/her to check up on. The time should be open to talk about almost anything. Aaron and I discuss things such as lust, jealousy, dating and sarcasm.

Accountability is vital for almost all of the things we've discussed in this book.

Focus on what's important. If you haven't washed your car in eight and a half months and you haven't had your devotions today, do what's important. Have your devotions. If your car's waited this long, another hour won't hurt. Pray that the Lord will reveal how to prioritize your life so that you will do what He wants, not necessarily what you want.

Write, baby, write. Speakers at motivational training seminars often address time management. Some of their stuff is good; some is unrealistic. One man said he stays about two months ahead of schedule. (I'd like to see me try that.) But one thing almost every speaker mentions is to write down the things you need to do. You have a lot better chance of remembering things if they're recorded in ink.

A lot of people carry a daytime planner. I write my list on note cards. Doing that has saved me from having to apologize for my forgetfulness a lot of times.

Pray about this part of your life and God will provide what you need. I've learned that the more you plan, the more you reflect peace. So go do it! Get yourself organized! You can manage your time and get more out of your day!

Never

again will convenience rule my life because I am committed to the cause of Christ.

WILL THE REAL ENEMY PLEASE STAND UP?

Some time ago I watched the final match of Wimbeldon, a prestigious tennis tournament. One player had fallen behind. I noticed she was talking to someone after each volley.

This confused me until someone explained that she was talking to herself. She had acquired the habit of reasoning with and encouraging herself during the game. She understood that though the opponent was very real, another obstacle prevented her victory—her own attitude. She had learned the mental discipline of fighting negative emotions as well as her opponent.

It worked. She won the match.

In the same way, our battle is not only against the unseen forces of Satan. We also fight someone we know quite well—ourselves. Here's why. When we trust Christ as our Savior, we are actually born a second time. We're born spiritually. This new birth doesn't mean, however, that our sin nature no longer exists. It's still there, but now it has some competition. The natural man, the flesh, wants to live as selfishly as ever, while the new nature wants to please God. Which wins?

> "So I say, live by the Spirit, and you will not gratify the desires of the sinful nature. For the sinful nature desires what is contrary to the Spirit, and the Spirit what is contrary to the sinful nature. They are in conflict with each other, so that you do not do what you want." Galatians 5:16-17

Every time there is a struggle between two evenly matched opponents, both sides take a beating. That's why we fight such an emotional battle. One side of us wants to do things the Lord's way; the other side wants to hold on to its own way.

That two-faced way of life is miserable. We will

become slaves to whatever we give in to the most.

> "Don't you know that when you offer yourselves to someone to obey him as slaves, you are slaves to the one whom you obey—whether you are slaves to sin, which leads to death, or to obedience, which leads to righteousness?"
> Romans 6:16

We will have constant inner turmoil until the new nature becomes more dominant than the old.

> "But thanks be to God that, though you used to be slaves to sin, you wholeheartedly obeyed the form of teaching to which you were entrusted." Romans 6:17

Becoming a "slave to righteousness" gives you greater freedom than you ever thought possible. The old, sinful part is still there. But for every wrong decision, there is a right one. For every negative desire, there is a positive step. For every ounce of strength of the old nature, there is the unlimited power of God to overcome it. On a moment by moment basis, which nature are you yielding to? When faced with a choice, ask God's Holy Spirit right then to give you the wisdom and strength to surrender to the will of God.

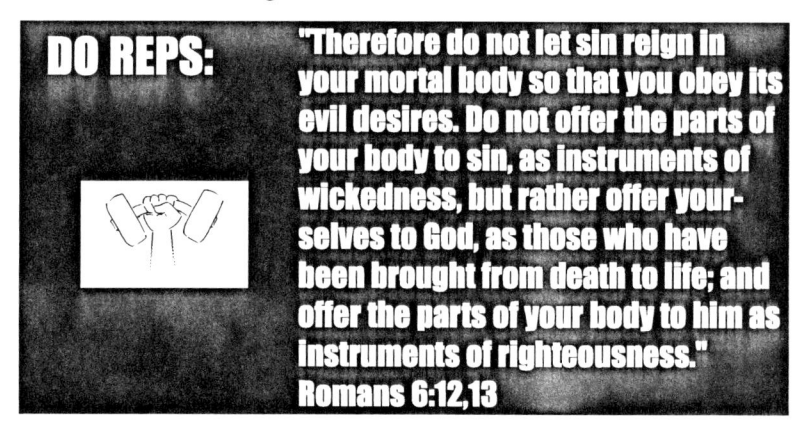

DO REPS: "Therefore do not let sin reign in your mortal body so that you obey its evil desires. Do not offer the parts of your body to sin, as instruments of wickedness, but rather offer yourselves to God, as those who have been brought from death to life; and offer the parts of your body to him as instruments of righteousness." Romans 6:12,13

kick

something out of your life that's messing up your christianity.

TIME IS MONEY

Imagine you get a call one day. "Hello," says a dignified voice, "This is Ernest Greenback, president of the Great Day Bank, and I've got good news for you!"

"What's that?" you ask suspiciously.

"Well," Mr. Greenback continues, "You've been selected for a special promotion. We've taken the liberty of opening a checking account in your name, and each and every morning for the rest of your life, your account will be credited with $86,400. You may spend it in any way you choose. However, at the end of each day, whatever you have failed to use will be canceled. No balance will be carried forward from the previous day."

After picking yourself up off the floor, what would you do? I don't know about you, but I'd figure out a way to draw out every cent—every day!

Actually, you do have such an account. It's called time. Every morning it credits you with 86,400 seconds. Every night it rules off whatever you have failed to invest. It carries no balance. It allows no overdrafts. You can't draw from tomorrow's assets. You have to live on today's resources. Doesn't that great potential deserve some careful consideration?

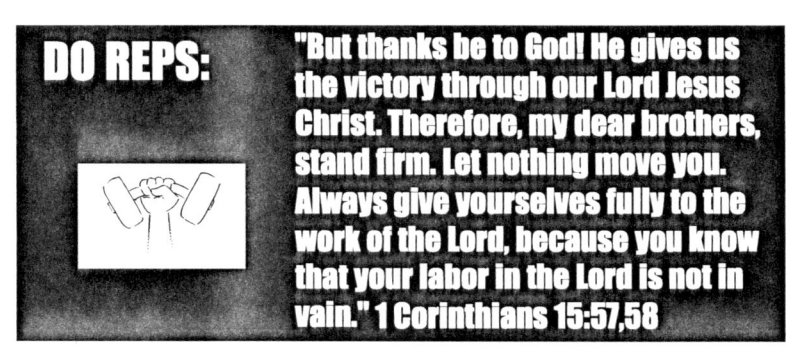

DO REPS: "But thanks be to God! He gives us the victory through our Lord Jesus Christ. Therefore, my dear brothers, stand firm. Let nothing move you. Always give yourselves fully to the work of the Lord, because you know that your labor in the Lord is not in vain." 1 Corinthians 15:57,58

GOD'S MEN ARE ORGANIZED

Four times in the opening chapters of the book of Joshua, we read that Joshua "rose early" to carry out God's instructions. (See Joshua 3:1; 6:12; 7:16; 8:10) He may have felt some trepidation about his assignment, but he was diligent. Joshua 11:15 says,

> *"As the Lord commanded his servant Moses, so Moses commanded Joshua, and Joshua did it; <u>he left nothing undone of all that the Lord commanded Moses.</u>"*

Joshua wasn't flashy, and he wasn't perfect, but he faithfully obeyed God. He led the children of Israel across the Jordan to the miracle of Jericho, forging on to fight enemies and subdue the land. Then began the methodical job of dividing the land so that each tribe received its inheritance. The fact that it was done peacefully reveals Joshua's leadership and organizational skills.

At the end of his life, he stated:

> *"Now I am about to go the way of all the earth. You know with all your heart and soul that not one of all the good promises the Lord your God gave you has failed. Every promise has been fulfilled; not one has failed." Joshua 23:14*

Joshua was a trustworthy man, passionate about God's people and God's work.

LOST FOREVER

A classified ad read, "Lost, somewhere between sunrise and sunset, two golden hours studded with sixty diamond minutes. No reward is offered, they are lost forever."

Is that about par for you, wasting two or three

hours a day in ten or fifteen-minute segments? "No, my time is completely filled," you say. Yet at the end of the day you have the feeling that you accomplished very little. We have some suggestions. We warn you, though, don't try them unless you really mean business.

It may take a while to get organized, but God cares about this part of your life.

So take a deep breath. Here we go.

DIALOG

DECIDE THAT YOU WANT TO BE ORGANIZED

When I decided that I wanted to be organized, I realized what a huge undertaking it was. But I was so tired of losing things, forgetting appointments, and making people mad at me that I had to try something. I still have a long way to go. No, I mean it... a really long way. But if you could see where I was before, you'd say I have already made progress.

You have made a lot of progress. Now you remember to check the oil in your car. For me, being organized comes more naturally. But since God has shown me that He's a God of order—just look at the Universe—I think we should try to reflect that order in our lives. Thankfully, the Holy Spirit is available to give us the strength and wisdom we need.

DON'T GET SIDETRACKED

A multitude of little things are going to get in your way every day to throw your schedule out of balance. Don't let them. Be flexible, but don't be a jellyfish.

Getting and staying disciplined means using your creative energy to stay focused. Do the stuff you don't enjoy when your energy level is highest. Something as small as letting your answering machine take your calls if you have a deadline can be the difference between grief and accomplishment.

At college there are a million things going on to get me sidetracked. When it's time for me to get some work done I have to go to a place where I know I won't be distracted. The people who get you sidetracked rarely have your best interest at heart. Where are they when you turn your paper in late?

BEGIN IN SMALL WAYS

"Someday I'm going to get organized." I've said that a million times. I realized that I needed to actually take steps. For instance, I was always bad about returning phone calls (still am sometimes), but now I make a list and twice a week, I sit down and return all my calls. I've also learned to have a spot by the door where I put things I need to take with me when I go out.

I find it helpful to tape up notes to myself to remind me of people to call and places I have to be. Plus we have a bulletin board in our house where we put all the urgent stuff that is temporary—the tickets for the ball game next week, someone's basketball schedule, a flyer for an event next month. Lots of people don't have a place for that stuff and wind up losing it. Little things like that can cause stress.

HAVE A PLAN

My mom tries to motivate me with sports analogies. She tells me to play offense, not defense, so I try to do that with my time. My day used to be decided by the people who would drop in on me at the last minute. Now I try to protect certain parts of my day, ensuring that I have time for devotions and promises I've made.

I think time should be budgeted just like money, including time for fun. I've learned that unorganized people don't really enjoy their lives because there is always something cluttering their minds. If a person can make a list each day and get two or three important things done, they will make steady progress. Unrealistic perfectionists stifle themselves; they see the perfect finished product, fear failure, and do nothing.

chaos

CHAOS

can be diminished with a simple plan and a little discipline.

SETTING GOALS

When I was in the eighth grade, my sister Julia, who is six years older than I, began dating a guy named Chris. Chris lived two hours away, so he'd come up every now and then and stay for a weekend. He and my sister would hang out, watch movies, and do whatever...and so would I! I loved to sneak up behind the couch and make faces until they turned around and looked at me. Then I would die laughing while Julia rolled her eyes. I was such a dork! I was also a major tag along, and I thought Chris was the greatest thing to ever hit the world. He was in college, a good athlete, and had a full-time job as a youth minister. In my eyes, he never messed up, even though he had the freedom to do whatever he wanted.

When Chris would come, he would play Nintendo with me when he should've been spending time with Julia. On a couple of occasions he invited me back to his town to hang out with his youth group. He even bought me a Christmas present! I couldn't believe he cared. Most guys that my sisters dated didn't like me hanging around.

That summer, Chris took all five kids in my youth group with his church to camp. At that camp, Chris encouraged me in my relationship with the Lord. He would always patiently listen to what I had to say, then speak grace into my life. I thank the Lord for him and consider him a godly mentor when I needed one.

I was reminded of Chris recently as I was preparing for a talk I was going to give to my youth group, which has grown considerably. I was reading Paul's first letter to Timothy. Timothy, who was a pastor, looked to Paul like I had looked to Chris—as a mentor.

Sure, Timothy was no eighth grader, but he must have been a young man because in 1 Timothy 4:12, Paul writes to Timothy, "Don't let anyone look down on you because you are young, but set an example for the believers in speech, in life, in love, in faith and in purity." Paul first says, "Hey, man, God has a special calling on your life. Don't back down because you're not as old as some people in your congregation." Then he tells him to "set an example for the believers."

Now the word *believers* means *saved ones*, or those who have accepted Christ. If you are young and a believer, this verse is telling you that you, despite your age, can have an influence on everyone. Does this include older people and adults in your church? Yes, sir. How about other kids in your youth group? Absolutely. It even means your parents and brothers and sisters at home.

So how do you set an example? We'll come back to this verse in 1 Timothy, but first let's look at another letter Paul wrote. In Titus 2:7-8, Paul says, "In everything set them an example by doing what is good. In your teaching show integrity, seriousness and soundness of speech that cannot be condemned, so that those who oppose you may be ashamed because they have nothing bad to say about us." Here it is—right here Paul is detailing the way to set an example. It struck me as odd at first that this verse used the word *seriousness*. Now I've never really been a serious guy, so this word immediately made me defensive. I wondered, *Is Paul trying to tell Titus that he's got to turn into some uptight guy who never smiles at anybody?* Hardly. This is the same Paul who wrote, "Be joyful always." He was not telling Titus to have a serious demeanor but instead to set serious goals for himself and to take his responsibility with other peoples' lives seriously. These words—"showing integrity and soundness of speech," plus the words of 1 Timothy which say "in speech, in life, in love, in faith and in purity," add up to make the formula for example-worthy living.

Maybe now you're calling me a dreamer and telling me that it's impossible for anyone to be so perfect that they set a perfect example for believers and non-believers both. Hold on. Nobody ever said it was going to happen right away.

Part of setting goals is taking them one at a time. For instance, if you bench press 150 pounds, and you want to do more, you do not set your goal to bench 275 in two weeks! No, you work to gradually get stronger, showing improvement each time. For those of you who aren't into weightlifting, I'll use the illustration of playing the guitar. When you first pick up the guitar, you don't just start playing your favorite song. You have to learn one chord, then two, then eventually, a whole song.

When I gave this talk to my youth group, we began by speaking something out loud that we wanted to change. It wasn't just getting rid of something negative, but replacing it with something positive. We said, "I don't want to be the kind of person who _____, instead, I want to be the kind of person who _____." For example, I said, "I don't want to be the kind of person who is sarcastic with other people, instead, I want to be the kind of person who is loving towards others." The youth group responded enthusiastically, and it gave them one tangible thing to focus on as they left that night. Why don't you stop right now and fill in the blanks with a goal you desire for your life?

ONCE YOU'RE THERE

You're fully conditioned and ready for service. How do you maintain an organized balance in life?

Always keep your word. When you make a commitment, do it. Don't be flippant about what comes out of your mouth. Weigh your words. Be a trustworthy person (Psalm 15:4; 19:14). Don't make promises to people that you can't keep. You can say no. People will respect you once they know you mean what you say. Your yes means yes. Your no means no.

See your work as God's assignment. (1Timothy 1:12, 6:20) Wherever you are right now—that school, that team, that job, even if it's temporary—is God's calling for you. You honor Him, you worship Him, you glorify Him by doing it as if you are working for God Himself. He will give you energy, skill and creativity as you pray over it. See it through. Finish well.

Be balanced. Don't let your schedule keep you from people. Develop a keen sensitivity to the needs of others. Few people intentionally distance themselves from someone whose words, facial expressions and mannerisms say, "I care." Look into people's eyes and lean toward them just a little as you listen. This says, "You have my attention, and what you're saying is worthy of my time." Carefully and prayerfully seek to help meet the needs of those you talk to.

Include Sabbaths, solitude, and fun in your schedule. God is so balanced, and we tend to be extreme. Why are really disciplined people hard to get along with? They are often inflexible and sometimes incapable of relaxing. If we reflected the true character of God, we would be orderly and full of joy and life. As we surrender to God, He stabilizes our *lives.*

God has created you for a high purpose. It will take inner strength—God's strength—in order for you to live His life. It's not about gritting your teeth and making rules. It's about having an all-consuming desire to live God's way.

At some point in your life, you are going to have to get off the couch and just do it. Stop giving all the reasons why you can't live for God. Decide to start taking the high road in life. Get the support you need and move forward. Start today in one small thing.

Seek to do God's will.

Nothing more.

Nothing less.

Nothing else.

DAILY MAXIMS FOR CONDITIONING

- I am now being built up and strengthened in Christ. Colossians 2:6

- I rejoice that Christ is at work in me to break old patterns of thought and action. Philippians 2:13

- The life I am now living is Christ's life. Galatians 2:20

- I am overflowing with thankfulness. Colossians 2:6

MAXIMUM CONDITIONING
MAXIMUM KNOWLEDGE
MAXIMUM FAITH
MAXIMUM DESIRE
MAXIMUM GRACE

CHAPTER SIX

Maximum Perseverance

Years ago, several of my high school buddies and I jumped in our old surf-wagon on a windy Friday afternoon and headed for South Beach in Miami for a weekend of great surfing. A small hurricane was churning up the Atlantic just a couple of hundred miles away, sending some awesome waves toward shore.

We hopped out, grabbed our boards, and plunged into the swelling surf. Good waves usually come in sets of three. My friend, Scottie, caught the second wave in a set and I caught the third one, a ten-footer in a big hurry to make shore.

There are no words to describe the thrill of surfing a big, powerful wave. Scottie and I both cut right, hollering at the top of our lungs at the ride we were having.

Suddenly, wipe-out! My mouth was still open and I found myself gulping salt water. While I was propelled toward the depths, my surfboard shot up in the air like a missile. As it twisted downward, the wind blew it right at Scottie who was still whooping it up with his great ride. I surfaced just in time to see the point of my board nail him on the side of the head, barely missing his temple.

The impact knocked Scottie off his board and split his ear. I felt like I was going into shock, but I had to save Scottie who was barely conscious. Somehow, I got him to shore and dragged him onto the beach.

Blood covered his face. Help came, and we got him to the hospital. We spent half the night in the emergency room waiting for the doctor to sew him up. Around three in the morning, we finally settled down in the back of the surf-wagon for some sweaty shut-eye.

Great, I thought as I tried to sleep, *I've sure blown this weekend. Scottie gets to sit on the beach with a major headache and watch me enjoy the best waves of the year.*

Next morning, we were out on the beach at sun-up. Big, beautiful, long-breaking waves rolled into shore. I looked up at the beach. Scottie was gone. I figured it was too much torture for him to watch.

A few waves later, I noticed a guy surfing with a ladies bathing cap on. *Funny way to surf,* I thought. Then I did a double take. It was Scottie! He'd put extra tape over his stitched-up ear, (hopefully to keep any trace of shark-calling blood out of our surfing area), bought a bathing cap, taken a couple extra pain pills, and grabbed his board.

He caught a good wave, shouting like a wild-man. I can assure you, I didn't surf anywhere near Scottie the rest of the weekend.

As I think back on our persistence as surfers, I'm amazed. We drove all the way to Miami with five dollars each to eat on and just enough gas money to get home. We slept in our wagon and fought off sand fleas all for the thrill of surfing. And not even a head full of stitches stopped us.

It makes me a little ashamed of the lack of commitment I see in Christians today. The first problem, the first disappointment of the day, and we're out of it, too busy licking our wounds to even get in the battle for God.

Let's do the opposite. Let's be so determined to serve the Lord that no inconvenience, lack of money, or physical setback can keep us off the front lines, fighting like warriors for the cause of Christ.

I had a friend who was persistent like Scottie, only his name was Brady. I met him in the weight room my junior year in high school. For me, as a fairly tall, skinny, eleventh grader, the weight room was the last place I wanted to be. Within the walls of that dreaded place were people who made me feel weak and powerless. Yet, that is where my coaches required me to be every day from one to two o'clock.

The first day of weight training class was humiliating.

The coach announced that we would be appointed workout partners based on our strength. He paired me with Brady, who weighed about thirty-five pounds less than I did (which wasn't much) and was almost a foot shorter—the smallest guy in class. Talk about feeling weak! He was the size of a fourth grader. And the fact that my coach thought of me on the same strength level as this kid was enough to make me want to quit. But I decided to stick it out. I figured Brady didn't want to be there any more than I did.

I didn't know I was about to learn a great lesson on work ethic. I attribute a significant amount of my baseball success to what Brady showed me about working hard.

From the beginning, I noticed Brady was an intense, fanatical weight lifter. He worked from the minute class started until the minute it ended. The guy wouldn't quit! I couldn't let him leave me behind, so I followed his lead. Before long, I'd put on ten pounds of muscle, my bench press level had increased fifty pounds and my squat had increased over one hundred pounds! But I still couldn't match Brady.

He didn't get any bigger, but he turned out to be one of the strongest guys in that class. What that guy lacked in natural size he more than made up for in perseverance.

DECIDE TO STAND IN THE GAP

God says He's constantly searching the whole earth for someone who will stick with it, someone He can trust for the difficult and thrilling tasks He has in mind.

> "And I looked for a man among them who would build up the wall and stand before me in the gap on behalf of the land so I would not have to destroy it, but I found none." Ezekiel 22:30

God is still looking for people today who will build a wall (live a faithful, godly, peaceful life) and stand in the gap (be an encourager and leader). Are you that person at your school? At your job? In your family? Don't be distracted by things our society says are important. God is with you, urging you to make godly choices.

> "What, then, shall we say in response to this? If God is for us, who can be against us?" Romans 8: 31

THIS IS YOUR LIFE

After my junior year of college, a friend and I decided to stay down in the Keys and earn money doing outdoor painting. We worked in the early morning and in the late afternoon. Because of the noonday heat, we spent the time after lunch working out inside and taking naps. Between the workouts, physical labor, home cooking and my tan, I went back to school looking good. Okay, I'll admit it, I was a hunk! Well, guess what happened to me after school started? I didn't have time for weightlifting. I didn't have my mom's good cooking. I lost my tan, lost the twenty pounds of muscle I had put on, lost my sex appeal. I was just Dale again. I wanted the muscle, but it wasn't a priority. The activities of my senior year of college distracted me from persevering in my fitness regimen.

A few years back I had a doctor tell me that I'd better start working out, because it would delay the progress of the kidney disease that I have. You know what? Now it's a priority. This is my life we're talking about! Of course, I have the same kidneys now that I had then. If I had realized how important it truly was, I may have kept working out all those years.

The point is, I see people, all ages, come to church and really enjoy it. They start learning and growing, and for about a year, they pursue all the things we've been talking about. But they do it to look good. They do it to feel good—making friends, feeling accepted all the things they did before, just in a Christian realm. They don't do it for the right reason, so they don't persevere. They don't realize that this is their life we're talking about! They do the "God things" to get what they want. But true joy comes from putting God's desires first...dying to our agendas and distractions. We will become steadfast when we understand that only God can give us what we need.

A DRIVING FORCE

A young student of Communism once wrote:

"There is one thing about which I am in dead earnest, and that is the Communist cause. It is my life, my business, my religion, my hobby, my sweetheart, my wife, my mistress, and my bread and meat. I work at it in the daytime and dream about it at night. Its hold on me grows and does not lessen as time goes on. Therefore, I

cannot carry on a friendship, a love affair, or even a conversation without relating it to this force which both drives and guides my life. I evaluate people, books, ideas and actions according to how they affect the Communist cause and by their attitude toward it. I have already been in jail because of my ideas, and I am ready to go before a firing squad."

Could this be said of you and me? It must be. Our cause is not a mere idea, but a person—Jesus Christ. Is He that important to us? We can stand on God's Word, no matter what comes against us. We can be victorious in Christ.

He gives us the strength to fight when we don't want to fight, fight when we think we can't fight any longer, fight when everything inside us wants to give up—that's perseverance.

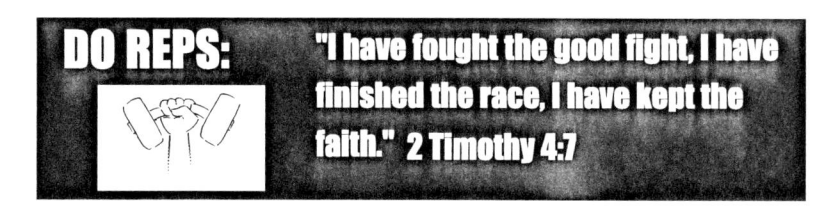

DO REPS: "I have fought the good fight, I have finished the race, I have kept the faith." 2 Timothy 4:7

DON'T QUIT

My baseball career hasn't been all that glamorous, but it has been fulfilling. From my first season of little league to this year, my last year of college, baseball has been good to me. But that doesn't mean it has always been easy or even fun. There have been numerous times when I've wanted to quit.

The first time, I was ten years old. My dad moved me up to the eleven and twelve-year-old league to give me a chance to play around guys with better skills.

Since I was trying to learn to switch-hit, I batted from the left side to let my skill from that side catch up with my right-handed swing. I probably had more strikeouts than hits! I batted seventh or eighth in the order, and my batting average was lower than my weight!

Things did get better. The next few years went pretty well. Then the summer after my eighth-grade year, I was asked to play on the varsity traveling team. I was extremely excited about it—until the first game. High school guys who didn't exactly like the idea of a thirteen-year-old on their team surrounded me. Plus, the coach's favorite form of instruction was yelling! I was totally intimidated, but I stayed on the team.

Going into my sophomore year of high school, I thought it was time for me to hang up the spikes. That was the year when I was ruled academically ineligible for baseball. I couldn't play, practice, or have any part on the team.

But then my parents and I figured out that I could get more individualized time with an instructor than if I went to practice every day. So I began to work out with a personal coach on my fielding, pitching and hitting. It was no substitute for playing, but it helped me stay motivated and kept me from quitting.

My junior year of high school presented more of a challenge than I expected, though. I had worked hard during the off-season. I was ready physically but found I wasn't wanted on the team! I had to work extra hard to prove myself that season, on and off the field. But it paid off.

The next year—my senior year—our baseball team was #2 in the state. My hard work and refusal to quit was beginning to reap results.

In college, another big challenge presented itself. I was pitching in a summer league after my freshman year and began to feel persistent pain in my arm. When I went to a physical therapist to get it checked out, an MRI revealed a partial tear of my rotator cuff. That meant surgery and six months rehabilitation!

This time, I thought, *it's a sure message for me to give up baseball and concentrate on my schoolwork.* I followed through, however, on what the Scripture says in James 5:14, "Is any one of you sick? He should call the elders of the church to pray over him and anoint him with oil in the name on the Lord."

I did, and God chose to allow my baseball career to continue! I went for a second opinion. This time the MRI showed no tear, but only a muscle weakness in my rotator cuff! Praise the Lord! That required extensive arm exercises with a Theraband and a one-pound soup can, but no surgery.

Going into my sophomore year, I was throwing again. Then about midway through the season, my pitching began to struggle. I'm talking major struggle! I couldn't get anybody out! It seemed like if I didn't hit a batter, I'd throw a pitch right down the middle for him to hit. For the first time since the beginning of my high school days as a pitcher, I was moved to the bullpen.

I was humiliated. I had pitched my way out of a starting job. I really wanted to quit, but I knew that wasn't the answer. Instead, I worked harder. I ran and did repeated drills to get my confidence back. The struggle continued for awhile, but eventually I earned my starting job back for the remainder of the season.

You'd think that'd be enough struggles for awhile. But after two starts in my junior year, I broke the thumb on my pitching hand. The therapist told me I would miss two months of baseball.

No way, I thought. *Surely a little broken thumb won't hold me out for that long.*

Again I had the elders pray, and again I went for a second opinion. But this time, the Lord wanted something else for my life. The second opinion was the same as the first. I missed six weeks of the season, which amounted to six starts. That was a long time for me to sit on the bench and watch everyone else play.

During that time, I still worked out, ran, and did my arm exercises so I would be ready to pitch when my thumb healed. It was awful doing all that work and not being able to play. I felt like I was accomplishing nothing. But the Lord was teaching me a lesson in perseverance.

Any athlete can tell similar stories. The road is not easy. It's long, hard and full of obstacles. I've practiced at 5:45 in the morning more times than I care to remember. I've done arm exercises with a one-pound soup can for three years. But when game time comes, it's all worth it.

Now it's game time for you. I don't know what your situation is—if you're facing a tough boss, a tough family situation, a tough physical handicap, or a tough relationship.

Whatever your game is, I encourage you to faithfully look to God for what you need, so you can look back one day and say, "I'm glad I stuck it out! I'm glad I didn't give up!" Ephesians 6:10-11 says, "Finally, be strong in the Lord and in His mighty power. Put on the full armor of God so that you can take your stand against the devil's mighty schemes." The devil was defeated when Christ died and rose again! Submit yourself to God and resist Satan in the name of the

Lord Jesus Christ!

Following the Lord is not always easy. But I encourage you to do it, whether it means changing friends, having fewer friends, or having no friends. Don't be afraid, and even if you are, do it anyway! Just as it says in Isaiah 41:10, "So do not fear, for I am with you; do not be dismayed, for I am your God. I will strengthen you and help you; I will uphold you with my righteous right hand." If you are full of fear, you can overcome it by living courageously.

You may be saying, "Easy for you to say, buddy. My situation is a lot harder than your little broken thumb." Believe me when I say the Lord will not give you anything you can't handle. 1 Corinthians 10:13 says, "No temptation has seized you except what is common to man. And God is faithful; He will not let you be tempted beyond what you can bear. But when you are tempted, He will also provide a way out so that you can stand up under it."

God is looking forward to the day that you come through your tough situation and you can praise Him. James 1:2-5 says, "Consider it pure joy, my brothers, whenever you face trials of many kinds, because you know that the testing of your faith develops perseverance. Perseverance must finish its work so that you may be mature and complete, not lacking anything."

Stand strong! Believe in the Lord! Keep standing! Just as Ephesians 6:18 says: "Therefore put on the full armor of God, so that when the day of evil comes, you may be able to stand your ground, and after you have done everything, to stand."

YOU

are stronger than you think you are.

ROCK SOLID

"Now it is required that those who have been given a trust must prove faithful."
1 Corinthians 4:2

This is the key to your Christian life: Be a rock. Faithfully follow God's commands. Even when things happened that you don't understand, don't quit. God is with you, ready to give you strength and courage for every burden, whatever it may be. When the situation looks hopeless, keep hoping. When everything looks impossible, refuse to accept defeat. Stay focused on Christ. He is your hope.

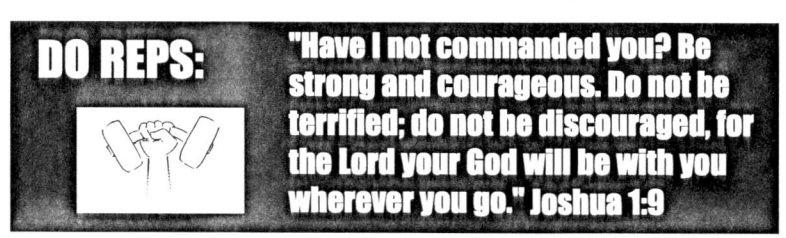

DO REPS: "Have I not commanded you? Be strong and courageous. Do not be terrified; do not be discouraged, for the Lord your God will be with you wherever you go." Joshua 1:9

That old expression, "to the bitter end," gives us a negative view of perseverance. We tend to think of it right up there with doing our homework. Look at what James says:

"Blessed is the man who perseveres under trial, because when he has stood the test, he will receive the crown of life that God has promised to those who love him." James 1:12

God tells us to persevere. He helps us to persevere. Then He gives us rewards when we do.

WHO'S EPAPHRAS?!

You may not have heard of Epaphras, but observe what kind of person he was from the three *times he is briefly mentioned in the New Testament.*

In Colossians 1:6 Paul commends the Colossian people for bearing fruit once they understood God's grace. Verse 7 says:

> *"You learned it (the Gospel) from Epaphras our dear fellow servant, who is a faithful minister of Christ on our behalf and who also told us of your love in the Spirit."*

Epaphras was faithful. *He showed up and he kept showing up. He lived what he believed.*

Then Paul mentions him again in Colossians 4:12,13:

> *"Epaphras, who is one of you and a servant of Christ Jesus, sends greetings. He is always wrestling in prayer for you, that you may stand firm in all the will of God, mature and fully assured. I vouch for him that he is working hard for you and for those at Laodicea and Hierapolis."*

Epaphras worked hard for those God placed in his life. *Even when he was not physically present, he "wrestled" in prayer for them.*

We see his name one more time in the book of Philemon, verse 23:

> *"Epaphras, my fellow prisoner in Christ Jesus, sends you greetings."*

Epaphras didn't wimp out when the going got tough. *Determined to persevere, he ultimately became a prisoner because of his faith.*

There will be days when you feel good about yourself and your life; there will be days when you don't. Days when you don't think anyone cares or anything you do really matters. On the days when you struggle, you will feel empty unless you focus on God and on encouraging others, persevering in the thoughts that you know are true. You then, like Epaphras, will be a reflection of Christ's life and a joy to others.

EXERCISE

your God-life every day.

DIALOG

WHEN YOU BEGIN TO WAVER, REMEMBER THESE THINGS:

GOD WILL GIVE YOU PEACE

John 16:33, Philippians 4:5-9, and Isaiah 26:3 are just a few of the many Scriptures that remind us to keep our minds on Christ. He will help us maintain our peace. But sometimes, instead of reminding ourselves that God is all-knowing and all-powerful, we allow our minds to be filled with hopeless thoughts, fearful thoughts, thoughts of resentment and anger. We turn into wimps, focusing on lies, lies, lies! It's time we change our perspective; instead of focusing on the problem, let's focus on God—He already has the answer. My problem is I plan the perfect day and the perfect life. Then when that doesn't happen, Ker-plunk! There goes my peace.

Oh, I've done that, too—plenty of times. I'll tell you something else that causes me not to have peace—plain old impatience. That, in turn, leads to anger. Let me give you a trite little example. When I'm getting ready for class in the mornings, I have to put my contacts on if I plan on seeing anything. Some days I have trouble getting them on. I find myself hitting the bathroom door, yelling as loudly as I can, pitching a fit. I can promise you it does nothing for my peace. What I should do is calm down and say, "Lord, you know I have to get these contacts in for class. Please help me." That doesn't mean a little prayer makes for a perfect day or a perfect life. But calling on God does bring peace.

GOD CUSTOM-DESIGNED YOU

Yes, Dad, I tell everyone we share a brain. Mom says we have flashes of genius with blank spaces in-between. But when I have those frequent blank spaces, I try not to get down on myself because I'm not perfect (really had to work on that one). I can rejoice that I am uniquely designed by God to glorify Him and He loves me just the way I am. When I realize that, I can begin to relax and enjoy my life.

It took me a while to learn that. I used to avoid telling anyone that I had a hearing loss. No wonder they called me "Fog". Then I read Exodus 4. God said to Moses, "Who gave man his mouth? Who makes him deaf or mute? Who gives him sight or makes him blind? Is it not I, the Lord? Now go. I will help you speak and will teach you what to say." So now I don't worry about my inadequacies. I can stand strong because God is not concerned about my hearing loss; He is concerned about my desire to hear His voice.

GOD WILL NEVER DESERT YOU

This was always God's answer to people in the Bible when they wanted to give up: "I will never leave you nor forsake you." They may have had good reasons for thinking they couldn't be strong, but God ignores excuses. His answer is, "Don't be afraid. I will be with you."

Why do we not believe that? Why do we act like it's no big deal? I know sometimes I forget that we're talking about the God who spoke the universe into existence. GOD. I don't ask for His help or acknowledge His existence. It's like carrying a candle around in your house when, at the flick of a switch, the whole house could be flooded with light.

Staying Power

On May 2, 1939, Lou Gehrig played his 2130th consecutive major league baseball game. Over a fourteen-year period, Gehrig had been hit in the head with a baseball three times, had surgery for a chipped elbow, broken the little finger on his right hand four times, broken six other fingers on various occasions, smashed the toes on his right foot, torn a muscle in his right leg, and wrenched his right shoulder. On top of all that, he was plagued by lower back pain. How could Gehrig play through all those injuries and never miss a single game? Perseverance—mental toughness. Nothing was going to stop him.

Theodore Roosevent said:

> It is not the critic who counts, nor the man who points how the strong man stumbled, or where the doer of deeds could have done better. The credit belongs to the man who is actually in the arena, whose face is marred by the dust and sweat and blood; who strives valiantly; who errs and comes up short again and again; who knows the great enthusiasms, the great devotions, and spends himself in a worthy cause; who, at best, knows in the end the triumph of high achievement; and who, at the worst, if he fails, at least fails while daring greatly, so that his place shall never be with those cold and timid souls who know neither victory nor defeat.

We are not responsible for results. We are asked to be faithful.

Live your life confidently, putting everything into God's hands. Exchange your strength for His. That is how you persevere.

You can't do it.

God can.

If you let Him,

He will.

Daily Maxims
For Perseverance

- I have been given a spirit of power, love, and self-discipline. 2Timothy 1:7
- God can take the messes I make and make something beautiful. Ephesians 1:11
- This temporary struggle is achieving for me an eternal glory. Corinthians 4:17-18
- I am assured that all things work together for good. Romans 8:28

MAXIMUM PERSEVERANCE
MAXIMUM CONDITIONING
MAXIMUM KNOWLEDGE
MAXIMUM FAITH
MAXIMUM DESIRE
MAXIMUM GRACE

CHAPTER SEVEN

Maximum Leadership

When I headed for home after my first year in college, I felt like someone had been holding my head under water and had finally released me to breathe. It was such a relief to get out of there! I had just gone through the worst year of my short life.

Don't get me wrong. I'm not blaming anyone at college. I made some really bad decisions, and I was desperately ready to change.

I came home with a game plan. I was going to surround myself with Christian friends from high school, shelter myself under my parents' wings, and relocate at a new college close to home in the fall. It was obvious to me that I couldn't handle myself well away from home.

Things went pretty much as I'd hoped. I lined up a school about an hour away from home, was plugging into my home church again, making better decisions, and beginning to grow in my walk with the Lord. I thought my plan was brilliant.

Then, very unexpectedly, a community college in Florida called to talk to me about a baseball scholarship. They remembered me from my senior year in high school and made me an offer I couldn't refuse. After much prayer, my family believed God had arranged this. So I agreed to go to school there.

I couldn't believe I was doing it, but after a great summer at home, I was going six hours away! So much for the brilliant plan.

As my parents and I headed down to Florida, a variety of emotions went through my head, but fear was the most prevalent. I was afraid of being the new guy again. I was afraid of leaving my comfort zone. And I guess I was afraid of slipping back into my people-pleasing ways. But regardless of how I felt about it, I was going. It was final.

We pulled up in front of my new home—an apartment that looked more like a cheap hotel in the woods than the nice place by the bay they had promised. I sat down on the bed and gazed around the room, confused.

Here I was, ready to test my newfound commitment. I knew the Lord was telling me, "If you want to prove that you can act like a Christian away from home, here's your chance."

"I knew I'd get the chance," I replied, "just not so soon!" When my parents left, I was alone in the apartment for a couple of days. I used the time to prepare for what was ahead.

Then the first of my three roommates, Nick, showed up.

Nick, a guy from up north, was someone who was not afraid to butt heads with people, and butt heads hard! We didn't exactly hit it off. However, we were forced to spend a significant amount of time together. First, he was my roommate. Second, he didn't have a car, so he depended on me for rides. Third, we were the only guys on the team who were not within driving distance of home. When the coach gave us weekends off, everybody drove home except Nick and me. Boy, those were some long weekends.

On a typical day, I'd get home from school, walk in the door, and Nick would start in, "What's your problem, Ben?"

"You don't like us, do you, Ben?"

"Ben hates us, Jeffrey (another roommate). Don't you, Ben?"

"Ben, give me the keys to your car."

There were a lot of ways I could have responded to Nick, but I really didn't know what to do. I'm talking absolutely no idea! Here I was, trying to show how a Christian acts, and all I wanted to do was cuss this guy out!

I remember talking to Dad on the phone. "I can't take this much longer, Dad. I want to do physical harm to Nick in his sleep."

"You can do two things," Dad said. I was excited! I had options! I figured one of them would be to come home! I was ready to pack my bags! But then he said, "You can pray for Nick, and you can bless him every day."

Oh, boy, I thought, *just great. That's easy for you to say.*

But he didn't give me another option. And believe it or not, the Lord helped me. As often as I could muster up the words and grit my teeth, I would pray for Nick. I also started to bless him every day.

If we had room check in our apartment, when I cleaned my room I'd straighten his up a little, too. If we went out to eat and he didn't have money, I'd pick up his tab. If he needed to borrow my car, I'd hand over the keys. I'd even wake him up for church on Sundays and make him come with me. I figured since we were the only two guys there on the weekends, we might as well go to church together.

No sudden change came over our relationship. At least not that I noticed. I went home for Christmas break, then grudgingly returned for the rest of the year. I can't explain how much I didn't want to go back. But what happened when I returned still amazes me.

Nick was a totally different person toward me! I can't remember him saying anything but compliments!

One day Nick, Jeffrey and I were sitting around and Nick said, "Ben, I know we've had our ups and downs, but you really are one of my best friends."

I wanted to say, *You call that ups and downs?! I call that a horrible nightmare!* But instead, I thanked the Lord and thought, *I was able to show grace to Nick because God gave me grace.*

1 Peter 3:9 says, "Do not repay evil with evil or insult with insult, but with blessing, because to this you were called so that you may inherit a blessing." Then verse eleven adds, "He must turn from evil and do good, he must seek peace and pursue it."

It's hard not to retaliate. It's hard to bless a person who's cursing you. It's hard to seek peace and pursue it. But that was my lesson. In the midst of that struggle, great things went on in my life and at that school.

A friend and I started a Bible study, and some of the athletes began to attend. I was going to a good church and becoming more consistent in my walk with the Lord. I was even becoming a spiritual leader on the baseball team. But I knew none of that mattered if I couldn't show love to my own roommate. Colossians 3:13 says, "Bear with each other and forgive whatever grievances you may have against one another. Forgive as the Lord forgave you."

This is a chapter about leadership. I hope every one of you becomes a strong Christian leader. Know this: solid leadership manifests itself in day-to-day relationships.

What if you're already a leader, maybe in your youth group, but you don't show respect to your parents or your brothers and sisters? Is that true leadership?

I stuck it out down there, and as hard as it was sometimes, I determined to act like a Christian. But what the Lord wanted, more than that, was for me to share His blessings with other people. In order for me to be a leader, I had to learn to bless one guy that I lived with and saw every single day.

The Lord wants that kind of leadership out of you, too. You can do it! It will change your life and bless you like you've never been blessed before!

WHO

can you bless today?

DO REPS: "Do everything without arguing or complaining, so that you may become blameless and pure, children of God without fault in a crooked and depraved generation, in which you shine like stars in the universe as you hold out the word of life." Philippians 2:14-16a

FROM PIT TO PALACE

Joseph was a teenager when God first gave him the dream of the leader he would become. Although he had some severe trials along the way, he eventually became second to Pharaoh in Egypt. Your trials will probably not be as dramatic nor your leadership as meteoric, but there are lessons to be learned from Joseph.

He was a leader wherever he was. In Potiphar's house he was "put in charge of the household." (Genesis 39:4) There, he prospered. When he was unjustly thrown in prison, he was "in charge of all those held in prison, and he was responsible for all that was done there." (Genesis 39:22) You may have difficulties at home, you may not like your job, you may wish you could go to a different school, but you can be a leader where you are. Bless the people around you. Glorify God with your life and attitude.

He was concerned about pleasing God and blessing people, not the other way around. Joseph could have avoided prison if he had been a people-pleaser, but then he wouldn't have been in God's place at the appointed time. We may go to church and bless God, then spend the rest of the week pleasing our friends. Rather we should seek to please God and bless others, even if they are diffi-

cult to get along with.

⊶ ***He was patient with God's timing.*** *Joseph eventually became Prime Minister, but it wasn't exactly overnight success. His attitude of blessing people is amazing when we consider he was in prison for thirteen years. Psalm 105:17-22 tells us how much responsibility Joseph was finally given "after the Word of the Lord tried and tested him." God knows how much and what kind of training you need along the way. Be patient and trust God's purposes. Many people who become leaders for the Lord never imagine themselves having the strength to influence others. People like Hudson Taylor, Amy Carmichael, George Meuller and D. L. Moody never specifically planned to be leaders in the Christian field. But what tragedy it would have been if they'd refused to be used of God.*

WHO AM I?

In the first church I pastored, I learned that God doesn't have a "preacher pattern" that we all have to follow. Being new to the ministry, I worked diligently to please others, to say the right words, do the right things, even wear the right clothes.

Needless to say, I struggled big time and the people under my ministry struggled, too. They didn't know who I was because I didn't know who I was. I lacked the strength to lead, because I wanted to make everyone happy instead of just trying to follow the Lord's leading.

In time, the church folded. I thought I'd really failed as a pastor and didn't ever plan to try it again.

But God is a God of surprises. Years later, God called me back into the pastorate. I had learned from my previous experience, and said, "God, this is going to be Your church. And I'm not going to be afraid to be different. I'm just going to be the person You created me to be."

Since then, it's been wonderful to see what God can do, even with an off-the-wall, creative, little-bit-crazy person like me.

God also made you with special plans in mind. No matter what your limitations, no matter what you've been through, God will use you. Don't be afraid to come to Him as you are. Norman Vincent Peale said, "Don't crawl into your hole. Live dangerously. Don't think you are going to live with joy and happiness if you live softly. Get into life! Wade into it! Throw yourself into it!" I love that! That's how I want to live. What about you?

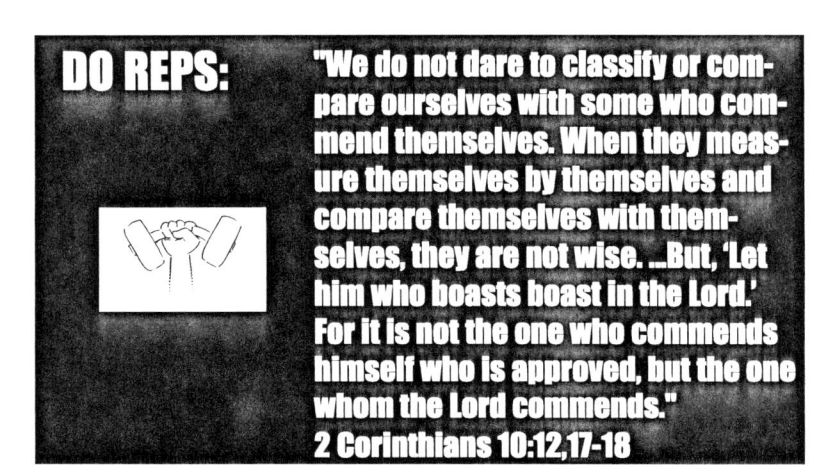

> **DO REPS:** "We do not dare to classify or compare ourselves with some who commend themselves. When they measure themselves by themselves and compare themselves with themselves, they are not wise. ...But, 'Let him who boasts boast in the Lord.' For it is not the one who commends himself who is approved, but the one whom the Lord commends."
> 2 Corinthians 10:12,17-18

Just

be yourself.

FOLLOWING THE STEPS IN REAL LIFE

My sister Natalie is a perfect example of what we have been talking about in this book. In her quest to find her calling, she started at desire and worked through each step on the way to becoming a leader. Let me tell her story, then I'll explain.

I told you that she was small and timid as a sixth grader, but the day she got her hearing aids, she made a decision. She wasn't going to spend her life crying about things she couldn't change. She began to have a desire for things to be different, and by being open about her hearing loss, she began to take risks—to have faith that with a different attitude, her life could be different. She didn't become a straight-A student, she didn't get perfect hearing, and she certainly didn't all of a sudden become athletic, but as she became willing to try new things, her life slowly took shape.

In seventh grade a teacher asked her to try out for cheerleading. She made the squad and found out she was really good at it. She started growing and gaining confidence, but she learned that team sports were not her thing. She would happily sit on the bench and fill in if they were short of players, but to put her in the game, well...

One day in a softball game she was put in right field and my sister, Julia, was in center. In the third inning a fly ball came out her way. As she had been told, she yelled, "I got it. I got it." Then realizing she had no clue as to how to "get it", she yelled, "Julia, get it!" Julia dove for the ball but came up short as it bounced off Natalie's shin toward the fence. They both rolled on the ground laughing uncontrollably while the left fielder ran all the way across the field to throw the ball in to third. Natalie's response: "I told the coach not to put me in the game."

At that point in her life, she could have quit athletics altogether. Instead she continued to be a cheerleader, becoming captain of the squad her senior year. In high school, instead of PE, she took weightlifting because she thought the girls in that class wouldn't be required to do much. She was wrong. She had a teacher—Coach Bishop—who believed that the girls in the class should work as hard as the boys. He was passionate about his area of expertise. Natalie began to ask him what workouts she could do to become a better cheerleader. As he explained more to her about the benefits of exercise, she caught some of his enthusiasm and worked to become a certified aerobics instructor her senior year.

When it came time for college, instead of choosing to become a kindergarten teacher as she had originally planned, she majored in physical education. She got her Bachelors in Physical Education, a Master's Degree, and is pursuing a doctorate. She is a teacher in our school system and also teaches college classes.

My other two sisters, Julia and Dawn, are extremely athletic. If they had become experts in physical education, it would have been no surprise.

The wonderful, amazing thing about this story is that if you had met Natalie in sixth grade, you would never have thought she had the potential to become what she is today. Every time she made a step in her life that moved her towards her goal, she worked through the steps that we use as chapter titles for this book. She had to have a desire to make a change; she had to believe she could do it. She didn't believe at the beginning for a doctorate one day; she just believed she could take a risk and go to cheerleading tryouts.

At each level she learned everything she could about what she was doing. Then she kept doing it because she knew that's how she would get better at it. She persevered. It didn't fall into her lap. She was willing to take jobs that weren't what she ultimately wanted just to get experience. It built her faith in her abilities.

You may think you don't have what it takes to become a dynamic Christian, but you can begin with desire and become an amazing story yourself of how God can do awesome things.

Chapter	Weightlifting	Life
Grace	Given a healthy body	Salvation is a free gift
Desire	Want to take good care of body	Because of God's gift, I want to live for Him
Faith	Believe weightlifting could bring results	Believe God can change my life/ core beliefs
Knowledge	Learn proper technique & helpful info	Learning truth, gaining wisdom
Conditioning	Get a plan of action/ go for it	Training self to daily obedience
Perseverance	Stick with the workout	Continued faithfulness despite difficulties
Leadership	Become instructor/ personal trainer	Passing on what I learn to others

DO REPS: "Whatever you do, work at it with all your heart, as working for the Lord, not for men." Colossians 3:23

I know of a girl who came to the Lord and wanted to serve Him with her life. She hoped to stop doing the self-destructive things she was doing. She got counseling, but she wanted overnight results and changes. She wanted to immediately fill all the voids left by her friends who were continuing down the road she was now avoiding. Waiting for answered prayer was too slow for her. When she said she wanted to serve God, her counselor said, "You have a wonderful personality for being a greeter in church. You could start there." She wouldn't. That wasn't what she had in mind.

I'm a pastor. Do you know how important I think greeters are in church? I would love to have someone take that on as his or her ministry. But often people won't begin where they are. They are too impatient to study the Word and wait on God to open doors for them. They want big results without taking small steps.

These chapter titles aren't a Biblical formula. They are attitudes that people need to cultivate in order to grow in their Christian walk and develop their gifts.

A VISION FOR YOUR FUTURE

*Ask God to give you a vision of what **He** wants your life to be...a vision so compelling that even when you make mistakes, you keep believing God is going to use you. Have faith in His power to overcome all of your fears and weaknesses. Ask Him to show you His love so clearly that you will live fully and passionately, in spite of your circumstances.*

If you begin using the talents, skills and spiritual

gifts that God has given you, you will become a leader. Start acting like the person you want to become.

There is a great day coming when Christ, who is our life, appears and we will appear with Him in glory (Colossians 3:4). We will stand before the King of kings and Lord of lords. He will ask, "Did you exult in My marvelous grace? Did you live up to your exalted status as one who was My child and heir? I gave you the highest of all reasons for living: to know and love Me, to show My love to other people, to glorify Me and to enjoy Me. Did you realize that you are one of My masterpieces?"

Will you bow down and smilingly say, "Oh, yes, Lord, what an honor. It was a delightful life because of Your amazing grace and Your love which You fully lavished on me."?

We invite you, we beseech you, we encourage you to make your life burn brightly.

Our Blessing For You

Be encouraged that God is saying to you as he did to Joshua:

> "No one will be able to stand up against you all the days of your life. As I was with Moses, so I will be with you; I will never leave you nor forsake you. Do not let this Book of the Law depart from your mouth; meditate on it day and night, so that you may be careful to do everything written in it. Then you will be prosperous and successful. Have I not commanded you? Be strong and courageous. Do not be terrified; do not be discouraged, for the Lord your God will be with you wherever you go."
> Joshua 1: 5,8,9

You are significant.
You are accepted.
You are secure in Christ.
Live joyfully as a liberated child of God.
Walk jubilantly in His love.
Max out on God.

Daily Maxims for Leadership

- I am born of God and the evil one cannot touch me. 1John 5:1
- Through Christ I am more than a conqueror. Romans 8:37
- I may approach God with boldness, freedom and confidence. Ephesians 3:12; Hebrews 4:16
- Through God's provision of grace I can reign in life! Romans 5:17

- MAXIMUM LEADERSHIP
- MAXIMUM PERSEVERANCE
- MAXIMUM CONDITIONING
- MAXIMUM KNOWLEDGE
- MAXIMUM FAITH
- MAXIMUM DESIRE
- MAXIMUM GRACE

High-Intensity Workouts

Work Your Way Through These
for Individual or Group Study

GRACE

- *How do we find forgiveness for all our sins? Read Acts 10: 43 and Galatians 2:16. Write out Ephesians 2:8,9 in your own words.*

- *Do you struggle with fear of death or thoughts of death? Read Hebrews 2:14-15 in various translations and write out your response.*

- *When you feel condemned or accused by the enemy, read Romans 8:1. Repeat regularly: "No condemnation!"*

- *Write out in your own words Psalms 103:8-12. Put your name in there.*

- *If you struggle with guilt ask the Lord to help you see the truth. Satan focuses on your feelings and accuses you. God focuses on your sin and forgives you. Which are you focusing on?
Read Zechariah 3:1-4. Memorize Romans 5:1,2.*

- *You have a choice. You can strive to make it to Heaven by your own efforts and try to be as good as Christ, or you can place your faith in Jesus and receive your right standing with God as a gift of grace. Make your choice now. To not do anything is actually deciding against God's gift. Write out or share your testimony with someone.*

DESIRE

- Read 1 Samuel 17. David was a teenager at this time. Write down "things David said or did." Write beside each item, something you can do in your life. (e.g. 1.David spoke encouraging words to Saul—I can be sensitive to my parent's struggles and speak encouraging words).

- List some things that you think make people like you. Go back and decide which are scriptural and which are not. What things are you willing to stop obsessing about?

- Write down ways in which God may have burned your ships. (no turning back). What are some positive things you may have gained from it?

- When you walk into a roomful of people, what do you say to yourself? Do you need to change that? Write out your new statement.

- Do the people you hang out with bring you up or down? How can you improve your relationships? (For example, share prayer requests, invite them to youth group.)

- Find the three qualities in the Desire chapter that are mentioned about Daniel. Write out a resolve for yourself.

- Is there someone that you share your truth with? What can you do to improve this?

FAITH

- In Judges 6:14 God says to Gideon, "Go in the strength you have—I'm sending you." What does that mean and how could it apply to your situation?

- Make a list of what you are struggling with today. Written out, it looks more manageable. Ask God for insight.

- What would you want to do in your life if you knew you could not fail? Read 1Timothy 4:14,15 and 6:20. What can you begin doing today?

- What are three lies you believe about yourself? Now from God's Word, what is the truth? Read Ephesians 1.

- In what ways are you a big baby? Is there a Scripture in this book that you can memorize to help you cope?

- What behaviors (or part of your appearance) are you or others trying to change? What are your core beliefs about these things? Do they line up with God's Word? Read Ephesians 4: 17-32.

- Write out one set of maxims and begin declaring those out loud every day.

- Share with someone three things God has done for you in the past. Give thanks.

- Have a private worship service today. Throughout the day declare, "My God is an awesome God!"

KNOWLEDGE

- *Is there anything in your life that you need to share with someone—some truth that you need to tell? Pray over it and ask God for a plan of action.*

- *What are three lies that you believe about God? From Scripture find and write out the truth about those three things.*

- *Get a devotional book/journal. Begin doing it as regularly as you can. Ask God to open your eyes to truth. Don't make it a guilt thing. Enjoy it.*

- *Is there an area of major struggle in your life? Look up and write out some verses about it and begin memorizing them. It may be hard at first but you can do it. God's word is powerful and worthy of our time.*

- *If you have doubts about what you believe, get a book to read. Don't make assumptions about the Bible, about God, about yourself until you've checked out the facts. (Josh McDowell books are good.)*

- *God wants people you meet to know the truth about Him. Decide that you will live the truth. Read Isaiah 1:16-17. What are some ways that you can bring God's truth to light in the places you go?*

- *If you truly believed that wisdom and understanding were more important than money, how would you change the way you live?*

CONDITIONING

- Read 1 Timothy 4:12 What is one thing in each area that you could do to move toward setting an example? (In speech—concentrate on being an encourager. In love—once a week do something kind for someone—wash your mom's car or take your sister somewhere.)
Write out "I want to be a person who ———————."

- What are areas of conflict that you have with your family? Jot these down. If Jesus was standing before you asking, "What do you want me to do for you?", what would your answer be? Make that your prayer request list for now.

- Think about your life/room/job/team. What are some practical things you can do to bring order? (Suggestions: Pick out your clothes the night before, including socks; get stuff together the night before—get papers signed, homework ready; buy two big plastic or wicker storage containers for your room and put all t-shirts in one, shorts in another; have a bulletin board, or a basket for temporary papers; straighten your room each night—not all day on Saturday; Sunday afternoon clean out your car as part of your schedule.)

- Decide when you will do your devotions. Then say to yourself, "If I had a class at that time or had to be at work at that time, I would do it. Shouldn't God be more important?"

- Pray for a mentor. Don't be afraid to ask someone if they would consider meeting with you. Who is someone younger than you that you could meet with and encourage?

PERSEVERANCE

▶ *What does it mean to persevere?*

▶ *Read Colossians 1:9-13. Write it in your own words. Paul prayed that they would have power according to God's glorious might (now that's power!). What was the power for?*

▶ *Do you have something in your life that has required great perseverance? How could these motivations apply to your Christian life? (Get yourself a spiritual coach, have a set time each day for doing it, etc.)*

▶ *Read 1 and 2 Timothy in "The Message" often. It's like having the Apostle Paul sit down and mentor you.*

▶ *Athletes understand that to be good they must train. Training hurts. It's tiring and it's hard. But an athlete who wants to win doesn't give up. What's important enough in your life for you to keep trying—even when it is hard or progress is slow? Read 1 Timothy 4:7. How do you "train yourself to be godly"?*

▶ *Write out a prayer expressing your desire to know Christ, to strive for what He called you to, to make living for Jesus your highest priority. Read Philippians 3:7-8. Write out and repeat often: "I consider everything a loss compared to the surpassing greatness of knowing Christ Jesus my Lord."*

LEADERSHIP

- It has been said, "The paradoxical truth is that I will never be happy if I am concerned primarily with becoming happy. My overriding goal must be in every circumstance to respond biblically, to become more like Christ. The by-product will be my eventual happiness." If you were more concerned about obedience than your own personal happiness, how would you act at home? At school? At work? What is one thing you can change right now?

- Make a list of three people that you are struggling to love. Pray for them each day. How could you bless them? Read 1Peter 3:8,9.

- Look at 2 Corinthians 10:12. Don't compare yourself to others. God made you just as you are for a reason. Write out three of your good qualities and add to the list as God brings them to your mind. Begin thanking the Lord out loud in your prayer time for things He has bestowed on you.

- Write out a Scripture prayer for yourself, inserting your name, and pray it faithfully. (Try Ephesians 1:15-19 or Ephesians 3:16-19)

- Joseph was a teenager when God gave him a dream for his life. It gave him confidence. Pray about your dream and your life purpose.

- What are some ways you can begin being a leader right now?

OTHER BOOKS FROM WISDOM PRESS

Max Out Growth Journal
Designed by Ben Crawshaw and edited by Jody and Becca Cheon, this unique devotional/guide is your opportunity to get serious about growing in grace and becoming the young man or woman God would have you to be. Pre-teens and older. Soft cover. $9.95
ISBN: 1-928554-04-0

The Best of Mind and Spirit
Dr. Robert Kamm, Christian statesman and former President of The Oklahoma State University, speaks with authority and passion in exhorting America to keep Christ in education. Hard cover. $18.95
ISBN: 1-928554-05-9

Reluctant Rainbows
Filled with encouragement from Dale's life and from the Scriptures, this book offers hope for anyone struggling with feelings of defeat, inadequacy, or hopelessness. Hard cover. $15.95
ISBN: 1-928554-00-8

Melvo the Parking Cone
Melvo the Parking Cone takes the reader through Melvo's eye-opening experiences as he gets his first big chance on the Utterback Construction site. He faces major peer pressure and sees the hurt it brings one wild cone. Melvo is then ready to ask the hard questions about peer pressure and friends. Based on a solid theme (taken from Proverbs 13:20)—and with colorful illustrations, too. Hard cover. $11.95
ISBN: 1-928554-06-7

Bone of My Bone: Journey to Reconciliation
Tony Hammon's story of reconciliation will give any reader hope to walk above the devastation of broken or abandoned relationships. Soft cover. $11.95
ISBN: 1-928554-03-2

The authors listed above are available for speaking engagements in churches, schools, and youth conferences. Pastors or youth workers may contact Wisdom Press for a complimentary copy of any one book.

Retailers may contact their favorite wholesaler or contact our distributor, FaithWorks.

FaithWorks' toll-free number is (877) 323-4550.

Wisdom Press
4540 Jot 'em Down Road
Cumming, GA 30040
(770) 781-5649
E-mail: juliafleming@ga.prestige.net